Dear Fellow Time-Binder

Letters on General Semantics

By Christopher W. Mayer

INSTITUTE OF GENERAL SEMANTICS

Copyright © 2022 by Christopher W. Mayer
All rights reserved. No part of this publication may be reproduced or transmitted in any form or by any means, electronic or mechanical, including photocopying, recording, or by any information storage and retrieval system, without permission in writing from the publisher.

Interior Book Design by Scribe Freelance
www.scribefreelance.com

Published in the United States of America
ISBN: 978-1-970164-16-9 (Paperback)
978-1-970164-17-6 (eBook)

Library of Congress Cataloging-in-Publication Data

Names: Mayer, Christopher W., 1972- author.
Title: Dear fellow time-binder : letters on general semantics / by Christopher W. Mayer.
Description: Forest Hills : The Institute of General Semantics, 2022. | Series: The new non-Aristotelian library series | Includes index. | Summary: "This is a series of short summaries and brief overviews of many main ideas within general semantics, all couched in the style of personal letters. It is designed to give people an intimate view into many insights offered with general semantics, and just as equally, it represents how principles of general semantics can be applied within everyday life"-- Provided by publisher.
Identifiers: LCCN 2022011699 (print) | LCCN 2022011700 (ebook) | ISBN
9781970164169 (paperback) | ISBN 9781970164176 (ebook)
Subjects: LCSH: General semantics.
Classification: LCC B820 .M39 2022 (print) | LCC B820 (ebook) | DDC
149/.94--dc23/eng/20220505
LC record available at https://lccn.loc.gov/2022011699
LC ebook record available at https://lccn.loc.gov/2022011700

BOOKS in the IGS Book Series
New Non-Aristotelian Library

Korzybski, Alfred (2010). *Selections from Science and Sanity.* (2nd Ed.). Edited by Lance Strate, with a Foreword by Bruce I. Kodish. Fort Worth, TX: Institute of General Semantics.

Strate, Lance (2011). *On the Binding Biases of Time and Other Essays on General Semantics and Media Ecology.* Fort Worth, TX: Institute of General Semantics.

Anton, Corey (2011). *Communication Uncovered: General Semantics and Media Ecology.* Fort Worth, TX: Institute of General Semantics.

Levinson, Martin H. (2012). *More Sensible Thinking.* New York, NY: Institute of General Semantics.

Anton, Corey & Strate, Lance (2012). *Korzybski and. . .* (Eds.) New York, NY: Institute of General Semantics.

Levinson, Martin H. (2014). *Continuing Education Teaching Guide to General Semantics.* New York, NY: Institute of General Semantics.

Berger, Eva & Berger, Isaac (2014). *The Communication Panacea: Pediatrics and General Semantics.* New York, NY: Institute of General Semantics.

Pace, Wayne R. (2017). *How to Avoid Making A Damn Fool of Yourself: An Introduction to General Semantics.* New York, NY: Institute of General Semantics.

Lahman, Mary P. (2018). *Awareness and Action: A Travel Companion.* New York, NY: Institute of General Semantics.

Levinson, Martin H. (2018). *Practical Fairy Tales For Everyday Living, Revised Second Edition.* New York, NY: Institute of General Semantics.

Levinson, Martin H. (2020). *Sensible Thinking for Turbulent Times: Revised Second Edition.* New York, NY: Institute of General Semantics.

Mayer, Christopher (2021). *How Do You Know?: A Guide to Clear Thinking About Wall Street, Investing, and Life.* New York, NY: Institute of General Semantics.

Levinson, Martin H. (2021). *Practical Fairy Tales For Everyday Living, Revised Second Edition.* New York, NY: Institute of General Semantics. (In Spanish)

For my friends at the Institute of General Semantics

Table of Contents

Preface 7
Letter 1: Time-Binding and Alfred Korzybski 9
Letter 2: Introducing General Semantics 13
Letter 3: Using Dates in a Process World 18
Letter 4: Indexing. 22
Letter 5: The Chain Index. 26
Letter 6: Etc. and the Principle of Non-allness 30
Letter 7: Introducing the Structural Differential. 33
Letter 8: Variations on the SD 40
Letter 9: The Map Is Not the Territory. 44
Letter 10: Fact-Finder 47
Letter 11: What's a Non-Aristotelian System? 55
Letter 12: Alfred Korzybski after *Science & Sanity* 62
Letter 13: Safety Devices 67
Letter 14: English Minus Absolutes 74
Letter 15: E-Prime 79
Letter 16: Either/Or. 83
Letter 17: The Meaning of Words 87
Letter 18: Operational Philosophy 93
Letter 19: Non-Additivity and True, False, Indeterminate, and Meaningless 99
Letter 20: IFD Disease: Idealism, Frustration, and Demoralization 104
Letter 21: Silence and the Delayed Reaction. 110
Letter 22: Logical Fate 114
Letter 23: How to Ask a Question 119

Letter 24: The General Principle of Uncertainty.....124
Letter 25: The Sapir-Whorf Hypothesis 129
Letter 26: The Observer and Observed 133
Letter 27: Causation 137
Letter 28: Fictions... or Abstractions..............140
Letter 29: Media Ecology 143
Letter 30: Does GS Imply an Ethics................148
Letter 31: Final Letter and Summing Up........... 153
Author Biography................................ 157
Acknowledgements............................... 157
Index..159

Preface

You may have had this experience before: You come across a set of ideas that just "make sense." They stick with you and make you want to learn more about them. They give you a fresh perspective on life, the universe and everything (as Douglas Adams would say). They help you solve problems. They liberate, entertain and educate. And, naturally, you'll want to share these ideas with other people with the hope that they may help them as much as they helped you.

This is the experience I had with the set of ideas called "general semantics." The tag "general semantics" does not do justice to the power of the ideas anymore than the word "dinner" would be fit to describe a wonderful meal prepared by a world-class chef. But this is what you will discover in the pages that follow.

In the pages that follow, I will share with you some of the ideas I have found most useful. I could've done this in any number of ways. Certainly, there are some excellent presentations of general semantics in various books and essays (many of which I will name). But I wanted to try something a little different. I asked myself, how might I teach a curious friend about these ideas?

So, I hit on the idea of writing letters. Admittedly, few people write letters anymore. But the idea of using letters to instruct has a long tradition, perhaps beginning with the letters of Seneca. The old philosopher clearly wrote the letters with a broad audience in mind, as a way to share the teachings of the Stoics.

In a similar way, I wrote the following letters to share the wisdom of general semantics. The letters are mostly short and conversational and—I hope—easy to read. May these letters inspire you to apply general semantics to your life. And may these ideas help you as much as they've helped me.

Letter 1

Time-Binding and Alfred Korzybski

Dear Fellow Time-Binder,

What is a "time-binder," you ask?

You and I are both "time-binders." And "time-binding" is the most distinctive—and arguably most consequential—ability we have. To explain what I mean, let me start with a story...

Picture this: During a battle in WWI, an officer rides a horse amidst a barrage of gunfire. His horse is fatally shot and, in the ensuing tumble, falls on top of him—crushing his pelvis and dislocating his left hip. Somehow, he pulls himself free and remains at the front, using his sword as a crutch.

Sometime later, a general, seeing him hobble in intense pain, orders the young officer to a hospital. There, doctors tie him down to a bed, sedate him, and put screws in his leg and pelvis. The pain is so acute, the officer decides to kill himself. But he doesn't even have the strength to reach for his gun. The injuries sustained leave him with a permanent limp. He would walk using a cane for much of his life thereafter.

That officer was Alfred Korzybski (1879–1950), fighting on the side of the Allies. And the transformative experience of the war helped propel him to develop a powerful idea: *time-binding*.

But before I get to time-binding, let me say a little more about this man Korzybski. (All of which comes from Bruce Kodish's excellent biography, *Korzybski: A Biography*.) I think it helps to know something of a thinker's life to give more context to his ideas. Korzybski thought so too. He once said, "Let me give you [some] advice when you read a book. Read not only what you read but study the author."

Korzybski was born in Poland to an aristocratic family. You will occasionally still see some people refer to him as Count Korzybski, even though he himself didn't use the title when he came to the US. He helped manage the family's estate from an early age, supervising up to a hundred workers in the harvesting season. He learned a lot about horses, breaking them in and becoming an expert rider.

Korzybski also received an impressive education. He learned multiple languages—his native Polish, of course, but also Russian, French, German and, eventually, English. Korzybski studied engineering as a young man. And he clearly loved mathematics, though he read widely across a variety of fields, devouring many books.

He came from a family of Roman Catholics, and his mother wanted him to be a priest. Korzybski himself would be agnostic on religion, critical of the dogma of both theism and atheism.

He migrated to the US in 1915, settling in Chicago. He married Mira Edgerly, a painter who specialized in miniature portraits on ivory. She would become an important partner for Korzybski's projects, providing inspiration and helpful criticism.

After the war, Korzybski would ask himself a question that would occupy his thinking for years: "What is the definition or defining characteristic mark of humanity?" In 1921, he published his answers in his first book, *Manhood of Humanity*. It's a good little book, relatively easy to read, thought-provoking, and quotable. And it has the core idea that would launch a much bigger project later.

In *Manhood to Humanity*, we see how Korzybski's early experiences shaped him. He writes warmly of mathematics and the methods of engineers. He writes about how engineers have to harness "natural laws" to bring ideas to realization. Engineers learn these laws through observation and trial and error. And he thinks a comparable thing should exist for the study of humanity—a kind of human engineering that brings together the sum of our scientific learning and applies it to the "advancement of human weal."

To create such a meta-discipline requires, Korzybski wrote, "candor, an open mind, freedom from blinding prejudice, thoughtfulness, a real desire for truth, and enough common sense to understand that to talk of adding three quarts of milk to three-quarters of a mile is to talk nonsense."

Idealistic impulses seem to drive Korzybski's vision, and the shadow of war and loss hang over the book's pages like a warning—a reminder that the cost of failure in this project could be immense. "The whole history of mankind," Korzybski wrote, "and especially the present plight of the world show only too sadly how dangerous and expensive it is to have the world governed by those who do not know [this contemplated art and science of human engineering]."

For Korzybski, the horrors of the war marked the end of childhood for humanity. Childhood was a period "devoid of any real understanding of human values," when humanity behaved like "a child who uses a priceless chronometer to crack nuts." Korzybski writes of the "wanton waste of life" and how we must not let the dead die for nothing—we must "make the future worthy of their sweat and blood."

In short, humanity must grow up. Thus, the "manhood of humanity."

(Better would have been something like "adulthood of humanity," but this was in 1921, after all.) To begin our life in adulthood, Korzybski thought it critical to understand what makes human beings different. In that difference we could discover the "nature of man" and find ways to live in accordance with that nature and allow humanity to prosper.

And here we get to his answer to the question: "What is the defining characteristic mark of humanity?" Korzybski found it in what people do, which other living things seem unable to do:

> Human beings possess a most remarkable capacity which is entirely peculiar to them—I mean the capacity to summarize, digest and appropriate the labors and experiences of the past.

We can read Plato and Galileo, Newton, and Darwin. We can pass on complex ideas across many generations. We inherit plans and recipes, a treasury of know-how and experience on which we can improve and create new and better plans and recipes. We are, in Korzybski's words, both an "inheritor of the by-gone ages and the trustee of posterity."

This capacity Korzybski dubbed "time-binding." Time-binding is what humans do.

This "mighty term" named the broad canopy that covered all the activities of human beings. Time-binding allows us to make everything from paintbrushes to stove tops, from golf clubs to bicycles. Time-binding allows us to publish books, to cure diseases, to build better homes and safer cars and bridges. Time-binding allows us to do more and more things, to explain more and more phenomena as the years go by. You might say the chief difference between human beings today and human beings of 500 years ago is that we benefit from 500 years of time-binding.

Time-binding fosters the flourishing of civilizations and the blossoming of individual potential. Time-binding allows human beings to make meaningful progress, amplified over time. As Korzybski put it:

> Civilization... is the process of binding time; progress is made by the fact that each generation adds to the material and spiritual wealth which it inherits. Past achievements—the fruit of bygone time—thus live in the present, are augmented in the present, and transmitted to the future; the process goes on; time, the essential element, is so involved that, though it increases arithmetically, its fruit, civilization, advances geometrically.

Korzybski's thesis was bold, though not entirely new. Others before him had similar ideas. But Korzybski coined the term "time-binding" and placed it at the center of his system.

Manhood of Humanity received quite a bit of attention in its day and put Korzybski on the map, so to speak. Remarkably, he had not written anything before—published or unpublished—in any language. When he wrote the book in 1920, he was 41 years old, already a mature and worldly man. Yes, the book is optimistic, at times arguably even naive. It can be repetitive and the language can sound dated— but these are also part of its charms. Korzybski's is a pioneering effort, a sketch, as he would call it himself, of a bigger project he hoped the book would initiate—the study of time-binding.

Many questions remained, as he acknowledged at the end of the book. What are the limits of time-binding? What practices does "clear and sensible" time-binding require? What tools should we use to improve our time-binding skills? Does time-binding imply a kind of ethics?

It would take another twelve years for him to formulate his answers. Then Korzybski would publish what would become one of the most important books of the 20th century. I can say his book certainly had a big impact on my thinking. But this letter is long enough. If you'd like, I'd be happy to share more of Korzybski's story and tell you about his magnum opus in a future letter.

In any event, I hope you'll agree, fellow time-binder, that time-binding is an important activity—the capacity to bind time seems to be what makes human beings... well, human.

Your Fellow Time-Binder,

Chris

P.S. The philosopher John Dewey (1859-1952) made essentially the same distinction as Korzybski at almost the same time, in his book *Reconstruction in Philosophy* published in 1920. "Man differs from the lower animals because he preserves his past experiences," Dewey writes in the first line of *Reconstruction*. We live in a world of "signs and symbols."

Korzybski digested and synthesized an enormous body of knowledge in his magnum opus. So, you will find many predecessors and antecedents of his work in the great philosophers and thinkers of the past. Korzybski's own work is time-binding par excellence.

Letter 2

Introducing General Semantics

Dear Fellow Time-Binder,

I'm glad you'd like me to continue with Korzybski!

I imagine Korzybksi must've cut a distinctive figure. Shaved head. Smoldering cigarette in cigarette holder. Thick Polish accent. That limp. That cane. He wore work shirts, open at the collar—apparently an eccentric choice at the time for an intellectual, as his contemporaries often noted. I attached a picture to this letter, so you can have a look.

Marjorie Kendig, who worked with Korzybski for many years, said he had a "peculiar style of lecturing, a non-linear method of developing his exposition." He used "shocking examples from his study of mental hospitals, from psychiatry, from his own experience with deeply maladjusted people, criminals, etc. to (as he called it) 'shake them up' and 'get under the skins' of the class." Sounds like fun to me. Kendig reports his face and hands would say as much as his words and diagrams.

For a time, he and his wife Mira had a pet monkey, a ringtail capuchin named Kiki. And then, later, a second monkey. Korzybski's biographer reports that he finished his second book with these monkeys on his lap. He seems to have been a colorful, eccentric character.

Anyway, as I say, I'm also glad to hear you'd like me to continue with Korzybski's big idea: time-binding. You'll recall, I ended my last letter with a bunch of questions. How to answer them?

Here we get to applied time-binding, which has its own name. Time-binding provided a foundation for Korzybski's envisioned field of study. "In its applied aspect," his biographer Kodish wrote, "Korzybski came to call his study—much to his and others' regret—'general semantics.'"

General semantics, or GS for short. The name may sound off-putting and vague and even academic-sounding. GS proponents admit ambivalence about the name and say it does not do the ideas justice. The name seems to foster misunderstandings as to what Korzybski's project is all about. Hence the regret Kodish refers to. But it also seems too late to change it now.

So what is it, exactly?

GS can be an elusive idea to summarize succinctly, partly because the name itself is not helpful and partly because it is a subject of great breadth and depth. Korzybski himself spent more than 800 densely packed pages, with a lot of math and footnotes, describing what it is all about. So, a definition won't encompass everything, but I can try to fashion one that captures the spirit of it.

The relationship with time-binding may be helpful to keep in mind: *If time-binding represents our ability to pass on ideas across many generations, then GS is the applied aspect of how we structure those ideas and how we can communicate ideas more clearly and evaluate them more sensibly.*

That's my bare-bones attempt, but let's go through some richer descriptions of what GS is all about from past teachers and practitioners.

One description I like comes from Wendell Johnson, who wrote a fine book about general semantics back in 1946 titled *People in Quandaries*:

> General semantics is not "the study of words" or "the study of meaning," as these terms are ordinarily understood. It is more nearly correct to say

that general semantics is concerned with the assumptions underlying symbol systems and the personal and cultural effects of their use.

I like how Johnson uses the phrase "symbol systems," because too many people seem to want to reduce GS to a discussion about only words—and their meaning and use. But "symbol systems" includes mathematics, signs, images, etc.—all fodder for GS.

Another good description comes from Robert Wanderer, a writer on GS for many years:

> General semantics is the study of the relationship between words and people, between symbols and behavior, between what makes "sense" and what sometimes prevents us from achieving the degree of "sense" we'd like. We're concerned with false assumptions, unseen blockages in perception, hidden confusions in evaluation, and other ways in which we sometimes fail to act as efficient, as sensible, as human as we might.

That's a pretty good catalog of GS's chief concerns. As you can see, it deals with potent stuff.

I am also partial to Bob Pula's description, included in his excellent *A General-Semantics Glossary*. Pula taught general semantics for many years and seemed a wise and affable fellow with a good sense of humor. Pula called GS "a set of propositions which. . . can serve as the best tool we humans yet have for making sense of the otherwise baffling buzz of stimuli, noises, 'movements,' etc. that beset us from every side in all our days."

To make sense, or at least talk/think less nonsense, gets to the heart of why study GS at all.

One more thoughtful description, from Irving Lee, another of Korzybski's students and the author of a good book on GS titled *Language Habits in Human Affairs* (1941):

> General semantics sets up systematically (1) the characteristics of life facts about which communicators must be aware, (2) the host of language habits which represent those life facts inadequately, (3) specific, usable and teachable devices by which to make language habits produce proper evaluation.

Evaluation is a word that recurs in the GS literature. The meaning of evaluation is simple—anytime you like or dislike something, you're evaluating, or making an evaluation. Anytime you form an opinion or do an analysis—

again, you're evaluating. Evaluation is verbal and non-verbal. It includes all your reactions, even "knee-jerk" reactions. It is something done by our whole organism in its environment—not just "thinking," not just "emotions."

(As an aside, Korzybski used the term "semantic reaction," abbreviated as "s.r." But people can get confused and think "semantic" refers only to language. It seems to me "evaluation" is practically synonymous with "s.r." and covers what Korzybski meant to capture with s.r. Also, adding this new term seems to complicate things unnecessarily. So, for the sake of simplicity, I won't use "s.r." In later years, Korzybski, too, seems to have mostly dropped "s.r." in favor of "evaluation.")

Evaluation gets to the heart of what Korzybski originally had in mind with GS. In Korzybski's seminar at Olivet College in 1937, he talked about how "semantics" comes from the Greek word for "significance," "value," and "meaning." So he thought, at the time, the term "general semantics" would be a good name for a "general science of values and evaluation."

What you find when you study GS is just how confused our use of symbols is and how this pollutes our ability to think in a rational and sane manner about the world around us. I'll be happy to share examples in future letters.

Another way to think about GS is as a system, or practice, that focuses the time-binding energies of human beings by improving our evaluations and helping maintain a healthy sanity in what can be a nutty world.

All of the above is a way to say: Time spent studying GS can be life-changing.

Consider what Stuart Chase wrote in his influential book *The Tyranny of Words* in 1938—a book still in print today. Chase was a student of GS. He wrote "a brief grounding" in these ideas "makes unreadable most political speeches, classical economic theory, after-dinner oratory, diplomatic notes, newspaper editorials, treatises on pedagogics and education, expert financial comment, dissertations on money and credit, accounts of debates, and Great Thoughts from Great Thinkers in general." And then he adds, wittily, "You would be surprised at the amount of time this saves."

I chuckled at that, but I have had a similar experience. After I had spent time studying it, GS seeped into my thinking and changed the way I look at everything. I can't take seriously most of what I find in political speeches, advertisements, the opinions of pundits, rumors, etc. There's so much abuse of language, symbols, math, and logic. I find such propaganda more amusing than anything, and I enjoy poking holes in such messages using the tools Korzbyski gave me.

GS also leads to new ideas and perspectives we would likely miss otherwise; it's no surprise, really, that a new perspective brings news insights. And GS also brings with it a certain equanimity when we must discuss ideas that other people tend to get very emotional about. In summary, GS is not an idle philosophy; you can apply it to your daily life. I'd be happy to show you how in future letters.

Korzybski would build out his system in his magnum opus called *Science and Sanity: An Introduction to Non-Aristotelian Systems and General Semantics*, published in 1933, twelve years after *Manhood of Humanity*. He almost titled it *Time-Binding* but changed it to *Science and Sanity* "practically on the eve of publication," Kendig tells us.

Korzybski chose to add Non-Aristotelian to the title—again seeming to needlessly complicate things, in my opinion—to distinguish it from Aristotelian logic. This is a point we'll pass over for the moment, but I'll come back to it in a future letter.

Also, I want to point out that GS has evolved since 1933. Later writers added new tools and explained existing ideas in different ways. The GS I'm presenting here is the GS I use myself and is infused by my own experience and ideas from other disciplines. GS did not spring fully formed from Korzybski in 1933, nor is *S&S* some kind of bible. To think otherwise would go against the spirit of his enterprise.

GS needs to continue to adapt to the changing world or risk becoming a sort of dead language—which would be a shame because the GS tradition is rich in useful ideas worth keeping around. Even as GS changes, the basic framework that Korzybski provided is still there and gives GS its distinctive architecture.

I would love to share some of the practical tools you can use to start applying general semantics right away. Korzybski called them "working devices."

Your Fellow Time-Binder,

Chris

Letter 3

Using Dates in a Process World

Dear Fellow Time-Binder,
    Yes, I'll introduce you to the first "working device" in this letter. You'll get a fuller picture of what GS is all about. To show you how to use this working device, let me set a scene for you first.

My wife and I hiked a trail in Gambrill State Park. Over a rocky path lined with witch hazel, mountain laurel and pitch pine, we weaved our way up Catoctin Mountain to a stone overlook at the summit called High Knob.

The slopes of the forested mountain were awash in fall colors, a mix of gold, orange, and red. The forest is always changing—and not just with the seasons. The actual composition of the forest is ever-changing. We see an enormous fallen tree, toppled over long ago. Younger trees take its place. We even find one very young pine tree—a perfect 3-foot-high Christmas tree—seemingly out of place, perhaps from a seed dropped by a bird from another forest. Black bears and other wildlife live in these woods. We hear the knocking of a woodpecker echo through the trees...

Though the mix of trees and animals changes, we still call it Gambrill State Park. It has a name, but it is quite a different place today than it was, say, at its dedication in 1934. No animal living today was alive back then. And how many plants and trees have grown and died since?

The forest seems a good metaphor, or microcosm, for the world of our experience, a world in flux, a world of process. In *S&S*, Korzybski wrote that all we needed to be convinced that "the world and ourselves are made up of processes," was to look at old photographs of ourselves, or places we've been, and see the change.

Wendell Johnson thought the idea so central to GS that he wrote: "Upon the foundation of the process-character view of reality the whole structure of general semantics has been erected... No other fact so unrelentingly shapes and reshapes our lives as this: reality, in the broadest sense, continually changes."

Think of the world as full of events, not things.

I am reminded of Buckminster Fuller. Bucky, as he liked to be called, was a fellow traveler in the world of GS. Many of his concerns echo Korzybski's. Bucky pointed out that "humans still think in terms of an entirely superficial game of static things." But "science has found no 'things'; only events. Universe has no nouns; only verbs." Bucky once famously said of himself, "I seem to be a verb."

Alan Watts, who wrote many wonderful books on eastern philosophy, put the same idea in poetic terms. He said: "a living body is not a fixed thing but a flowing event, like a flame or a whirlpool."

The implications of a process world for time-binding are profound.

For one thing, it means that no two things are exactly alike, because no event occurs in exactly the same way. Think of Heraclitus and his famous maxim about how you can't step in the same river twice. Really, you can't step in the same river even once, as water flows all around continuously, even after your first step.

And you yourself are constantly changing, even if only in small degrees from moment to moment. Over a longer period of time, you can see the cumulative effect of the changes more easily. Think of those old photographs again. I am not the same person I was when I was 20 or 40—and not only physically different. I have different ideas today, different views. I've experienced more events. I've learned things. And I've forgotten things.

For another thing, a process world means names and labels can be deceptive. You might have had a great meal at a particular restaurant five years ago, but the restaurant is ever-changing. Though it may be a "great restaurant" in your mind, it may not be so good today. We have all had instances in our lives where we went back to a place and had a very different experience than the first time we were there.

The same holds with people, too. I used to love baseball when I was younger. But I don't pay much attention to it anymore. Yet, when I occasionally meet an old friend of mine, I find he operates under the assumption that I am still that big fan he knew 25 years ago.

So, to foster better time-binding in a process world, what can we do? Korzybski suggested a wonderfully simple device: the date.

Here's how it works: For any idea or event, you put a date by it. So you could say, Gambrill State Park$_{\text{Fall 2020}}$ to place in your mind when I was there. You might go in the summer of 2021 and it will not look as I described it. Or that restaurant you loved back in 2000, you could say Charlie's BBQ (2000)— you don't need to use a subscript, though that's how most GS people use it. My friend could keep in mind that Chris Mayer$_{1996}$ is not Chris Mayer$_{2021}$.

Dating helps when you think about authors, too. Alan Watts in 1945, when he was an Episcopal priest, thought quite differently about certain things than Alan Watts in 1965, when he became a favorite of the counter-cultural revolution. So it might not make much sense to say "Alan Watts believed X" without a date, since he changed his views.

Korzybski's device gives you a nice question to ask (if only to yourself) anytime you hear someone say "[Insert name of famous thinker here] thought X, Y and Z." You can ask, "Did he or she always think that?" Perhaps you will uncover an interesting evolution in that person's thinking, which I find is often the case.

And don't forget to apply it to your own beliefs, etc. I find it liberating to date my own opinions and analysis. I can take a position in 2020, date it as such, and realize, as Korzybski said, such a position has "no element of semantic conviction concerning" 2021 or any other time. Dating makes clear my positions are not something I must defend or feel I "own." They are not valid for all time. They were the product of a certain arrangement that existed then and I am free to leave them where they were.

Dates help too with subject matters of all sorts. People will say things like "Medical researchers have determined...." But you can ask "as of when?" Because beliefs change. Think about medical beliefs in the 17th century. Back then, the ideas of Galen and Hippocrates prevailed. Their views on health centered on the four humors—blood, yellow bile, black bile, and phlegm. When they were in balance, so the thinking went, the body was healthy. Bad health stemmed from the four humors being out of balance. If you had a fever, for example, it was because you had too much blood—which was hot, after all. Your doctor likely recommended you be bled.

But medical knowledge in 1650 is not medical knowledge in 2022. I use an extreme example, but even medical knowledge of 2022 is not the same body of knowledge and common practices as 2011. We shouldn't expect it to remain unchanged. Nor should we criticize scientists and others when they change their views. We should expect it.

You will read the news differently now that you understand this device. For example, columnist Gerald Seib writes in his column in the *Wall Street Journal* about how Joe Biden ran for president in 1988. And he sets out a belief of then candidate Joe Biden. Then Seib makes this statement in the second paragraph of his column: "More than three decades later, of course, that same Joe Biden became president."

Joe Biden$_{1988}$ is not Joe Biden$_{2021}$. And Seib's entire analysis is compromised by this simple misevaluation. Trust me: you will see people make these kinds of misevaluations all the time, now that you know about it.

You don't have to go crazy and date everything, by the way. You have to use some judgment and apply a date when you think it might be meaningful to do so.

You don't even have to date things visibly—you can just do it in your head.

It probably helps to date visibly at first. But eventually it becomes second nature and you will just date things in your head. You'll read a text that says, "Physicists believe...," and you'll silently add "as of today." Or you'll tap out an email saying, "I enjoyed *Casablanca*..." and add "when I last saw it ten years ago." A friend will say they had a great time at Gambrill State Park—and you'll add "in the fall of 2020." You'll hear a talking head on TV say you should buy Apple stock, and you'll say to yourself "that's what he thinks today—but he may change his mind tomorrow."

So, that's dating. It's the first of our "working devices." We'll go through a few of these and you'll see how they fit together nicely. In contrast with many other GS texts you might read, I wanted to start early with the three working devices, for two reasons.

First, because Korzybski maintained that these three were the key to the system. As Harry Weinberg reports in his excellent book on GS, *Levels of Knowing and Existence*, "Korzybski was fond of repeating that if one could just learn to use these three in all situations, he could forget all general semantics theory and still have the most important part of the system."

Weinberg also adds that "theoretically" if we used the devices in all of our evaluations—really let them sink in—then we would never "indulge in the wrong kind of worry." That's a big promise. We'll see if you agree after we cover them.

The second reason I wanted to get to the devices early is because they are, in my mind, an important part about what makes general semantics distinct—a discipline worth preserving on its own, even though you can find its main ideas in other thinkers that predate Korzybski and in other disciplines today. The focus in GS is on practice—daily living—and Korzybski's devices are workaday tools.

Your Fellow Time-Binder,

Chris

Letter 4

Indexing

Dear Fellow Time-Binder,

You are right when you say our first device seems like common sense. Korzybski would agree. He often said the basic elements of his system (the devices) were "baby stuff." The insights seem obvious. . . and yet so many people make considerable thinking errors by ignoring them. Many of these can be harmless, but some of them can be quite harmful, even deadly.

In fact, Korzybski himself committed a particularly horrible thinking error—but, to his credit, he rooted it out. Kodish, in his biography of Korzybski, quotes extensively from a letter Korzybski wrote to his friend and mentor, the mathematician Cassius Keyser, in 1920. I was shocked to read Korzybski railing against the "Jews." Here is a sample: "The Jews remained parasites, and they had to be such, the productive element was lacking in them." And it goes on for a full page!

How could Korzybski hold such a prejudice? This is the man who created GS—a system of practical thinking which exposes the irrational foundations of such prejudices.

Well, we can use our dates here, can't we? Korzybski$_{1920}$ was not Korzybski$_{1933}$ when *S&S* came out. As Kodish points out, Korzybski used this letter as a cause for self-evaluation. He "consciously examined and turned against these views."

The end result being that after 1920, in his letters and published work, there is "no trace of the Jew-hatred contained in the Keyser letter." And Kodish notes that throughout his life thereafter, he wrote about Jewish people with sympathy and even became an outspoken critic of the Nazis. Quite a turnaround for someone expressing the views he did in that letter.

Korzybski conquered his prejudices. Though we don't know the exact process he went through, I'd say it's a good bet he began to wonder about the good interactions he had with individual Jewish people and set these experiences against all this other awful nonsense he spewed out in his letter.

At the root of such prejudices is a basic fallacy: you take a label applied to certain people and make sweeping generalizations about them. GS has a "working device" that makes such generalizations impossible to maintain.

Korzybski called it the "index."

Here's how it works: Say I am listening to a friend disparage "immigrants" as "criminals" after he reads a story about an immigrant robbing a store. I could ask him "Are all immigrants criminals? What about our Vietnamese barber? She's one of the sweetest people we know." Unless he's particularly irrational, he's going to have to concede that not *all* immigrants are criminals and yes, he likes our Vietnamese barber too.

What I've done here is take a blurry label ("immigrant") and instead focused it on an individual person—a tangible and observable event of experience. From such small cracks in thought, even tough prejudices begin to crumble. The immigrant who robbed the store is not the same as the immigrant who cuts your hair. As a GS person would write: immigrant$_1$ does not equal immigrant$_2$. Or mentally, when we hear someone talk about an "immigrant" would silently amend the word to read "immigrant$_1$," or "immigrant$_X$"—the "x" denoting a variable than can change, as used in mathematics.

The use of subscripts—the index—remind us that no two things are exactly alike, even though they may share the same "class," or verbal handle or symbol. As with the date, you can make the adjustment in all your reading and writing—and speaking and listening, too. I find using the index helps remind me to question labels and classes. Such distinctions are made up. They are human creations and they don't exist in the world "out there."

We rely on labels all the time, and often they are mostly harmless. For example, consider: "Canadians are polite." All Canadians? Safe to say probably not. Canadian$_1$ is not the same as Canadian$_2$, Canadian$_3$, Canadian$_4$,... Even so, such prejudice is not likely to cause much harm—perhaps only surprise when you run into a "Canadian" who exhibits rude behavior! But sometimes prejudices can be quite hurtful indeed, such as prejudices against Jews, immigrants, Muslims, gays, etc. Use of the index here reminds you to think of individuals. The index reminds you of differences whether others see similarities. No two people are exactly the same. Baby stuff, right?

I can recall lots of examples from the financial world where use of the index might've made you quite a bit of money—or cost you money, depending. Commentators are apt to refer to businesses in broad categories—"tech stocks," "retailers," "airlines," etc. The implication being that all such businesses in these categories are all basically the same.

I had a friend who had a bias against "oil stocks." He had lost money on oil producers before. And to be frank, many oil companies have been bad businesses in recent years and oil executives have made bad decisions—at great cost to their shareholders. To my friend's way of thinking, oil stocks are all the same—oil stock$_1$ = oil stock$_2$ = ways to lose money.

But I had discovered a stock called Texas Pacific Land Trust (TPL), which owned land in west Texas, in the oil-rich low-cost Permian Basin. It was an unusual "oil stock" because it didn't produce any oil itself. No risky drilling or heavy capital investment, which usually hampers returns in "normal" oil companies. TPL has other companies extract the oil, incur the expense, and take on the greater risk. And in return for using its land, TPL got a royalty, typically 1/16th of whatever the value of the oil extracted.

It was (and still is) a beautiful business. And that stock would eventually increase in value by over 5x in less than a year. But my oil friend never really gave it any thought. In his mind, it was an "oil stock" instead of an "oil stock$_1$" . . . and so he missed a big gain.

Another favorite example is when the McDonald's franchisor of South America went public. Called "Arcos Dorados" (Spanish for "golden arches"), it had 1,770 restaurants throughout South America. At the time, there were over 14,000 in the U.S. alone. Wow, what growth potential! Anybody wants to open a McDonald's anywhere in South America they have to go through Arcos Dorados. Investors loved the story and bid up the stock. Unfortunately for them, they did not consider that McDonald's$_{\text{In the US}}$ is not McDonald's$_{\text{In South America}}$. There were cultural, legal, economic, and geographical differences. And these differences mattered. The business struggled through many challenges, and the stock lost over 80% of its value in the next five years.

Baby stuff, right?

To sum up: The index reminds us that no two events ("people," "things," etc.) are exactly alike. And the date reminds us that the world is ever-changing. You can even use both the date and the index for the same event—such as "oil stock"$_{\text{1 circa 2020}}$ and even expand to include location ("oil stock"$_{\text{1 circa 2020 in the US}}$). The nuances are endless, but remember to assess whether you need the index. The devices have great power when used judiciously.

Using these two devices, you start to get the essential pieces of GS and your time-binding skills have already increased. But we have more devices to cover...

Your Fellow Time-Binder,

Chris

P.S. Labels are slippery at best. In this letter, I assume we agree on, say, what a "Canadian" is. But what is a Canadian? Someone born in Canada? What if they left when they were two years old and never returned? What about someone born somewhere else, but who grew up there? The point is, these terms have fuzzy edges. We throw around words as if we know what they mean—"birds," "chairs," "cars," "Mexicans," etc. Even something so simple as a "tree." But what is a tree?

As it turns out, it is not so easy to define what a tree is, as Rachel Ehrenberg wrotein the article "What Makes a Tree a Tree?" published in *Knowable Magazine*. There is no trait that exists only in a "tree." Ehrenberg quotes geneticist David Neal, who says: "Trees are big, they're woody, they can get water from the ground to up high. But there does not seem to be some profound unique biology that distinguishes a tree from a herbaceous plant."

Tree seems easier to define as a kind of event, instead of a "thing." And here I would like to quote Ehrenberg's words because they so neatly echo what we covered in our last letter: "Maybe it's time to start thinking of tree as a verb, rather than a noun — tree-ing, or tree-ifying. It's a strategy, a way of being, like swimming or flying, even though to our eyes it's happening in very slow motion. Tree-ing with no finish in sight — until an ax, or a pest, or a bolt of Thanksgiving lightning strikes it down." Remind you of Buckminster Fuller? "I seem to be a verb," Bucky said. And Korzybski, too, by defining human beings not with static attributes (opposable thumbs!) but with what they do—time-binding.

As I mentioned in an earlier letter: there are no things, only events. Trying to define events precisely is like trying to tie down clouds or hold on to a stream. Think of events in terms of what they do, what their effects are. Events are better defined by movement and change. Good time-binding takes this into account.

Letter 5

The Chain Index

Dear Fellow Time-Binder,

I agree that "context is everything," as you say. Although, I think the context goes even deeper than you may imagine. Events—"people" "things"—always exist in an environment, in space and time (or space-time as a GS person would say—but more on that later). These connections are so strong that I find it hard, if not impossible, to imagine otherwise... though, again, our language can lead us astray.

I am reminded of a simple, wise Indian sage named Nisargadatta Maharaj (1897-1981). From his "humble tenement in the back lanes of Bombay" (in the words of his translator Maurice Frydman), Maharaj would hold court with visitors seeking his advice and wisdom.

Maharaj grew up in a poor family and had no formal education. And yet, his sparse, clear teachings cut through the assumptions we take for granted in everyday life. One of the ideas he stressed over and over again is that everything connects with everything else.

"No thing in existence has a particular cause," he said. "The entire universe contributes to the existence of the smallest thing; nothing could be as it is without the universe being what it is." Nothing exists by itself.

The idea of a separate "you," then, is a sort of illusion. There is no "you" without a place to stand and air to breathe, for example. You need the food and water you consumed. So now you're talking about a whole long trail of crops and animals and sunshine and rain. And you need parents. And your parents need parents. And on and on it goes, bringing in many, many people going back in time. You need the universe.

Where does the "you" begin and end? Usually, we think of the dividing line as "inside our skin" and everything else is "outside of our skin"—a "skin-encapsulated ego," as Watts used to say. But even here, outsides only exist with insides. It is impossible to imagine either without the other. As Maharaj would say, you are different but not separate.

The idea that "you are one with everything" may seem mystical, but then Einstein$_{\text{February 1950}}$ thought much the same thing:

A human being is part of the whole, called by us 'Universe'; a part limited in time and space. **He experiences himself, his thoughts and feelings as something separated from the rest—a kind of optical delusion of his consciousness.** This delusion is a kind of prison for us, restricting us to our personal desires and affection for a few persons nearest us. Our task must be to free ourselves from this prison by widening our circle of compassion to embrace all living creatures and the whole of nature in its beauty. Nobody is able to achieve this completely but striving for such achievement is, in itself, a part of the liberation and a foundation for inner security." [emphasis added]

Strong words for something almost everyone seems to take for granted: the idea of a self separated from a whole, existing in itself.

This may be a strange way to kick off this letter, but it does serve to introduce another "working device" called a "chain index"—a kind of ancillary working device to the index. Call it working device "2b." Yes, believe or not, we're not quite done with the index yet.

The chain index can get tricky to explain. Kodish writes it has "significantly bedeviled generations of students of Korzybski's work." But there is a very good example I'll use to show you how it works—inspired by a similar example used by Francis Chisholm (a skilled teacher of GS from the 1940s).

Let us take the example of my iPhone. Sitting here in my office, I get fine reception. However, not long ago I was on a remote stretch of highway, tucked between mountains—with the "same" iPhone—and I got no reception at all.

Here is where the chain index comes into play. My iPhone $_{\text{in my office}}$ is not the same as my iPhone $_{\text{on that remote stretch of highway}}$. I mean, it seems the same. We talk about my iPhone as if it was the same phone. But the chain index reminds us that environment matters—place and time matter (or can matter). Remember, to think of events in terms of what they do, not in terms of static attributes. In this case, the iPhone works differently in different settings. GS teaches us to incorporate that into our idea of the iPhone.

This is where it bedevils students, because people want to say it's just context. For example, when in Nicaragua years ago, I enjoyed drinking a beer called Toña. Sitting by the Pacific Ocean at the Rancho Santana resort with the salty sea air and warm sunshine... in that setting, an ice-cold Toña tasted fantastic. But I remember my friends and I once bought it stateside. It was terrible. This is what we liked to drink? Well, the context is important. I know people who say Guinness tastes better in Ireland and Pernod better in France. And Ouzo... well, it still tastes terrible even in Greece!

But you see the difference in these examples, right? With the iPhone, I'm still talking about something we would say is the "same" just in a different location. But the chain index doesn't apply in the beer example, because in both cases I'm drinking from an entirely different bottle of beer.

Tricky, yes?

Of course, you could account for time and place using the index we talked about in the last letter. So Toña$_{\text{in Nicaragua}}$ is not the same as Toña$_{\text{in Maryland}}$. I'd say that's a helpful use of the index. GS emphasizes that things exist in an environment. In fact, there is an oft-used phrase in GS circles—"organism-as-a-whole-in-its-environment"—that emphasizes this point. I just want to be clear that the chain index makes a somewhat different point. It's not only that thing$_1$ in environment$_1$ is different from thing$_2$ in environment$_2$. It's that every thing$_x$ is different from itself in a different environment.

Not everything needs a chain index. Sometimes it doesn't really make a difference. If my iPhone operated in the exact same way all the time in every place, then there is no sense in thinking about a chain index.

As Kodish says, "with the chain index, we make our own little chain reaction of differences, of differentiating one thing in our classification or naming, so one thing becomes two things or more depending on the context of time and place (although the time dimension can be taken care of with the device of dating). Further differentiating as to context, can go on indefinitely, although it is probably often not necessary."

And this brings me back to the beginning of this letter, when we talked about the self. The idea of a stable and separate "you" is a kind of illusion, as the Hindu sage Nisargadatta Maharaj taught. Gad Horowitz, author of *The Book of Radical General Semantics*, also raises the question what we mean by "self". Sounding a lot like Alan Watts, Horowitz writes that we can make no absolute distinction between "outside the skin" and "inside the skin"—because the chain index makes the environment part of the defining feature of a self. You can't pull out a "self" absent of these things. There is nothing to extract.

Further, think about how we act quite differently depending on the context we find ourselves in. We do not behave the "same" at work as we do at home. We behave differently with different friends. We behave differently in different environments. We are different from ourselves.

As Horowitz explains, the chain index prevents us from mis-using the index. It doesn't allow us to imagine a unique indexed individual that "contains its existence within itself, a simple, isolated, atomic, thing-in-itself, identical to itself, that it exists *essentially* as a substance outside of any environment or context, as if it could enter into, move or be moved from one context to another and 'go through' many changes without ceasing for a moment to be what it 'is' essentially."

Events have no essences; they are movements. Events are ever-changing happenings unfolding in space-time. As Bucky says, you seem to be a verb.

Your Fellow Time-Binder,

Chris

Letter 6

Etc. and the Principle of Non-allness

Dear Fellow Time-Binder,

There is one more device you should know about. It will complete the trio of "working devices" Korzybski thought these three were the key to his system. You now know about the date and the index. Next, I want to introduce you to the "etc."

The etc. expresses another key pillar of GS: the principle that you can never say (or know) all there is to say (or know) about any event. The principle is called *non-allness*. And Korzybski called "etc." the "junior infinity."

The idea is so important that the Institute of General Semantics (founded by Korzybski in 1938) chose to name its quarterly journal *ETC*. Korzybski used it so often in *Science and Sanity* that he came up with six abbreviations for "etc."—which seems to me to be a mistake in presenting his material. The quirky punctuation does nothing to add to anybody's understanding of the device. But it does make *S&S* even harder to read and needlessly complicates the text.

I think you can safely ignore these abbreviations and just use the "etc." pretty much the way people conventionally use it. You add "etc." to the end of a description to show that there is more to what you're saying.

What makes GS different here is that we deploy it a lot more often. We recognize no matter how rich and detailed any description seems, there is always something left out. Maybe what's left out is not important. Or maybe it is. The etc. reminds us to think about it.

Again, you don't have to be a zealot about it. Prudent use of the devices heightens their power, while thoughtless use weakens them. As with all devices, they don't have to be visible. You can mentally make the adjustment. (Of course, in speaking, you have no choice.)

Korzybski famously used a pencil to make his point in *S&S*. It's an effective example because a pencil is such a simple "thing." Surely we can nail down what it "is." Well, grab one and let's see. (Another one of Korzybski's pet phrases was "I don't know. Let's see.")

Now, look at the pencil, feel it, weigh it in your hands... You could describe its color, size, and weight. You could catalog little nicks and imperfections. You could comment on the eraser. You might comment on the materials and its construction. There is a lot you could say.

But Korzybski nudges us to think more deeply about this pencil. He adds we could think of the pencil as "a dance of 'electrons,' which is different every instant, which never repeats itself. . . [and is] acted upon, and reacting upon, everything else."

Well! If you really think about it, we can never capture what this pencil "is." There are countless details and ways of describing this pencil—and it's always changing. You come to see that we always leave things out when we describe a pencil—as we must and as we should.

As Korzybski says, the actual pencil is something "unspeakable." You can't capture an event entirely in words. In another oft-quoted phrase, Korzybski says "whatever you say something is, it is not." We can formulate descriptions, but those descriptions are not the actual event.

Of course, the description of a pencil may be inconsequential, but you can readily apply the same principles to any description. If a pencil is so simple and we have challenges there, think about trying to capture a person with words.

Consider filmmaker Robert Snyder's description of one of my favorite personalities from history: Buckminster Fuller (1895-1983). Snyder, who was Bucky's son-in-law, described him as:

> A sailor, a machinist, a comprehensive generalist, a doer, a new former, a student of trends, a technical editor, a businessman, an angel, a quarterback, a lecturer, a critic, an experimental seminarist, a random element, a verb, a comprehensive designer, an inventor, an engineer, an architect, a cartographer, a philosopher, a poet, a cosmogonist, a choreographer, a visionary, a scientist, a valuable unit, a mathematician, an air pilot, a Navy lieutenant, an affable genie, a geometer, a maverick thinker, a gentle revolutionist, a lovable genius, an anti-academician, doctor of science, doctor of arts, doctor of design, doctor of humanities, an amiable lunatic, a prophet, the custodian of a vital resource.

That's a long list of terms—and yet, there is a lot more one could say. (And the list itself contains descriptors that invite questions). Hence, a GS practitioner would add an "etc."

I don't limit the use of "etc." to descriptions of physical events either. Any summation of a theory, a book, a movie, etc. demands an. . . etc!

I love how the "etc." cultivates humility and a heightened awareness. It reminds us to handle descriptions with care. Perhaps paradoxically, it also takes some pressure off our own evaluations. We know we can't capture everything. So we make our best effort to get at what's important for the purpose at hand

and add an "etc." to cover omissions. It's simple, but don't underestimate its power to change how you think.

So, now you have the three key "working devices," as Korzybski called them. They will improve your time-binding skills. Use them. And let me know how they work for you.

Your Fellow Time-Binder,

Chris

Letter 7
Introducing the Structural Differential

Dear Fellow Time-Binder,

The devices do make a difference, don't they?

As I say, most GS books don't give you the "working devices" until later in their texts, after they've covered a lot of other ground. However, when I try to introduce people to GS, I like to bring the devices out early. They give people some quick, easy-to-remember, and easy-to-understand (and distinctive) ideas from the GS toolbox. And the devices then become part of a helpful vocabulary I can use to talk about the rest of GS with them.

Korzybski might've agreed with me. He introduces the working devices in the preface of the second edition of *S&S*. And he starts using them early in *S&S* itself, starting in the first chapter of Part I of the book, titled "The Preliminaries."

In any case, once I've shared all three, I like to line up each of the three devices alongside the perceptual challenges they seek to aid us in addressing, like so:

- We live in a world of process; nothing stays the same (that's why we use *dates*).
- No two events are exactly alike (which is why the *index* is helpful).
- We can never say or know all about any event (hence, *etc.*).

Remember, the term "events" covers "things," "people," etc.

As Korzybski said, with these three devices you have the bones of the GS system. But you will have a far richer experience—and a lot more analytical firepower—if you're willing to lay some additional bricks on top of this sturdy foundation.

What I want to do next is to introduce you to a diagram that captures the essence of all those three points—and much more. Kodish, Korzybski's biographer, wrote that this diagram "showed the mechanism of time-binding in its starkest, ideal form." And Korzybski himself thought it captured "the foundation on which all human activities are based." It's so distinctive and unique to GS that enthusiasts put it on t-shirts! People hang renditions of it on their walls. It crops up in all the books. And it's probably unlike anything you've ever seen before.

Korzybski called it the "structural differential," henceforth the SD. See the picture nearby. He created it in a fit of inspiration while giving a lecture, drawing it out on a blackboard.

Let me show you how it works.

At the top is the parabola, or event level. This represents everything that happens "out there." Sometimes GS teachers will refer to it as "what is going on" or WIGO. It's the whole swirl of sights, sounds, smells, and countless other details that are ever happening and changing, whether we pick up on them or not. It represents happenings outside *and* inside our skin (an important feature often forgotten). The dangling strings and many holes are meant to represent these many details. The rough edges along the top are meant to indicate the limitless characteristics of any event. You could think of the parabola as the raw material from which our perceptions come.

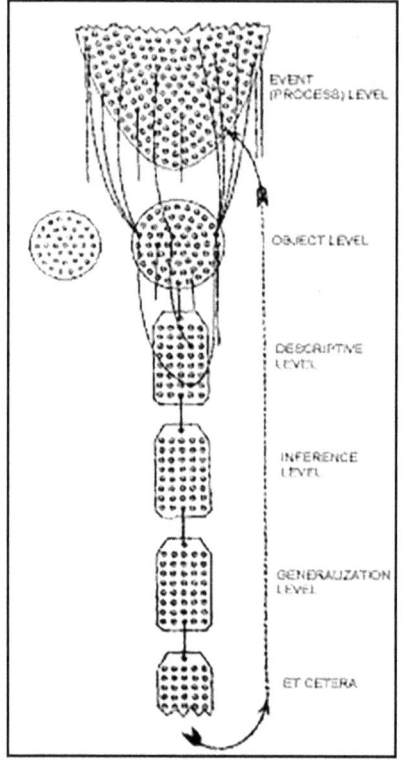

The next level down is the object level. You'll see it picks up *some* of the strings and has fewer holes. You also see that it is a finite size and smaller. The object level represents our drawing out perceptions from events. We don't take in everything. And the object level is still nonverbal.

The next level down is the descriptive level. This is smaller again than the object level. It brings even fewer strings and fewer holes—and takes on a different shape. Here we begin to put together our descriptions, which do not capture everything we've picked up at the object level. In any description, we pick and choose what we want to talk about or note.

The next level down is the inference level. Here we start to draw inferences from our description. No strings reach this level, which shows again how more details have been left behind.

Down another level takes us to generalizations, which we form from our inferences. Generalizations are really another kind of inference, so you could just say everything from this point on down is just another inference. And below that, we see an "et cetera" to mark the idea that we continue drawing up more inferences in a potentially endless number of possibilities (marked by the jagged edge at the bottom). We can always make another inference, another generalization, another statement about a statement, and so on. We don't ever have to stop talking—and some people don't, though we wish they would!

The arrow that brings the whole process back to the parabola, or event level, shows us how this process is ongoing. There's a feedback loop, a continuous flow of events, perceptions, descriptions, generalizations, inferences, ideas, theories, etc.

This process of moving down the SD is called *abstracting*. This is a key term in GS and refers to this process of how a human nervous system pulls perceptions from events and forms descriptions, inferences, generalizations, etc.

In GS circles, we talk about *lower-level* abstractions versus *higher-level* abstractions. Lower-level abstractions are closer to the event level. As we move away from the event, we form higher and higher level abstractions.

So, if you're on a boat and cry out "look!" and point to a dolphin cresting, that's a lower-level abstraction. We might characterize such abstractions as being dynamic, continuous, immediate and, as Korzybski would say, "above all *un-speakable*." We can perceive them before we have described them using language.

Once we start to use language, we move up to another level of abstraction—further removed from the event—into static analyzable descriptions. The higher-level abstractions are uniquely responsible for our time-binding. A higher-level abstraction would be to talk about, say, a poodle or a Ferrari or a professor. An even higher level abstraction would be to talk about democracy and free trade and money.

We ought to value the lower order abstractions over higher level abstractions. Korzybski talks about the *natural order of evaluation*, which goes something like this:

1. Event: physico-chemical, electronic processes, etc,—*are more important than...*
2. Object: non-verbal abstractions drawn by our nervous system—*are more important than...*
3. Descriptive: verbal descriptions—*are more important than...*
4. Inferences: lower level *are more important and more reliable than...*
5. Inferences: higher order, etc.

The higher we go, the less reliable our evaluations. Korzybski contended that most of us invert the order here and thus give undue weight to higher order abstractions. On reflection, this must be so. How else do you, say, get tens of thousands of young people to agree to risk their lives by going off to a faraway land to kill people they've never met? How else do you explain people getting in fights with other people who root for another football team? How else to explain people getting angry with someone because they happen to agree with a different political party? In all cases, people are putting a lot of weight on higher order abstractions.

I often will tell myself when some big election or other world event seems momentous: "I will still sleep in the same bed, live in the same house, eat the same food, have the same family and so on." I'm reminded of the comedian Bill Hicks and his routine where he watches the news and it's all about death, destruction, disease, etc. And then he looks out his window and wonders where all this stuff is happening. . . There is something to be said for the tranquility that comes with a Korzybskian orientation.

Korzybski hoped that once we see that words are not the thing, we will be careful not to confuse levels of abstractions. We wouldn't take a high-level abstraction, such as *democracy*, and objectify it, make it a thing like pointing to that dolphin. If we did, we'd risk becoming dogmatic, insisting what democracy "is." I think Korzybski's warning was apt. For example, a recent *Economist* headline for example reads, "How resilient is Democracy?" The question struck me as a confusion of levels of abstraction. Democracy is not a thing, but a high-level abstraction, far removed from what it aims to describe and thus an ambiguous term at best. Therefore, is it reasonable to talk about *democracy* as having a quality such as *resilience*? Or are there better questions we might ask?

Likewise, we can confuse lower-level abstractions and treat them as higher-level abstractions. If we treat that unique human being standing before us, who happens to be wearing a burka, as a "fanatical Muslim," then we risk unnecessary fear, pessimism, bitterness, and ignorance and a disregard of a scientific mode of thought more generally. Other animals don't seem to have this problem, which reminds me: I forgot to mention Fido.

See that little circle all by itself over there in the SD model? That's Fido, a dog. It's actually supposed to represent other animals in general. Korzybski originally had the inspiration for the SD when he was trying to convey his idea of time-binding and how this is a thing we humans do that other animals don't do.

So, Korzybski wanted to show how animals obviously have perceptions, but they don't do much with it, compared to us. They don't create ideas like *democracy* and *nation-state*. They don't dream up *Star Wars* movies or write poetry or decide to wear funny hats or build libraries or invent tax forms. Fido's abstracting powers stop well short of ours. "Fido has no science," Korzybski writes. Poor Fido.

This perceived difference from other animals, which Korzybski called "time-binding," seemed quite important to him. I imagine because the question of what a human being "is" was the big question that started his whole project, beginning with *Manhood of Humanity* back in 1921. (Perhaps ironic, given his warnings on the use of that word "is.")

But it seems less important to me sitting here in the 21st century, even a little quaint. When I share the SD with other people, I usually opt for a version without Fido at all. But I've included Fido here because perhaps you'll get a fuller picture of how the SD fits with Korzybski's views on time-binding—which is what we started our letters with.

Anyway, going through an example might be helpful in showing how the SD works.

Say I'm standing at the first tee at a golf course. Before me stretches the golf course in infinite detail—trees, grass, hills, sand, water, wind, sun, etc. Maybe I feel a little nervous. Maybe my shoulder hurts a little bit. And there are lots of other things going on inside my skin that I miss or can't pick up. (I'm not conscious of my digestion, etc.) All of this is WIGO—both outside my skin and inside—and is what we mean by the "event." I take it in, nonverbally.

But I don't take it all in. Think about the details such as blades of grass, leaves, etc. There are details I can't take in. And there are details I could, but will miss. In any event, I do pick up some details. In this case, I see a line of trees off the right-hand side of the fairway. I see a pond in front me. I feel the breeze blowing behind me. That's the object level, which is still nonverbal.

Now, we go down another level, and I start to make descriptions. I think to myself, the fairway looks pretty broad. The trees are in play. I feel pretty good today, shoulder not bothering me much, etc.

Then I make an inference. I should have no problem getting my ball over this pond.

I may then make a generalization from that inference: There is a lot of water on this golf course.

I may make yet another inference: This golf course is not easy.

I could go on for a long time. In fact, as I play the course, the event will constantly change before me, and so will the object level. I'll make repeated inferences. Some of them will be "wrong." I may think a putt is straighter than it is. (And when my ball rolls left of the hole, I'll know it.) All throughout the day, this process will be ongoing. If I played the same course the next day, it would be a new "event." Sure, there would be similarities—the big tree off the fairway on number 9 isn't likely to go anywhere. But there would also be differences—in weather, in how I'm hitting the ball that day, etc.

Assume I write an article about the golf course and get it published in *Golf Digest*. I give advice on how to play and share my inferences. Time-binding in action. Now other golfers can read what I wrote. They can then play the golf course themselves. The event will have changed, though. It won't be the "same" golf course, not exactly. And they will see things differently. They will make their own evaluations, their own inferences. Perhaps someone will write a different article, building on what I wrote. More time-binding.

As the months and years go by, the golf course will continue to change in many respects. Trees will grow. Some will die. Courses sometimes undergo re-designs—changing the distances between the tee box and the green, adding sandtraps or removing them, cutting down trees and planting new ones, etc. My descriptions over time will grow ever more distant from the "object" they initially described and the "event" from which they were drawn—or *abstracted*.

Using the SD reminds us of this process of abstraction. In every description, inference, generalization, etc. . . this process goes into their making, whether we make them or other people make them, whether we get them orally or by reading. And our biases, experiences, etc., come into play. We "symbolize" our experience only after they have passed through "a very thick layer of cultural cheesecloth," as Wendell Johnson put it.

The SD model is powerful and compact. It instills humility, because it shows you, in stark terms, how our inferences are far from the events from which we draw them. As Korzybski used to say, if you really understand the SD, you will never take a word (or a description) for granted. You will ask (if only to yourself) what is missing? Ever sunny about what GS could achieve—and the SD in particular—Korzybski$_{1924}$ said widespread use of the SD would "prevent publication of nine-tenths of books and the delivery of the majority of speeches, inasmuch as most of them are based on Fido-ways." Poor Fido, coming in for some abuse. (I note Korzybski wrote this in an early paper, delivered in 1924, called "Time-Binding: The General Theory.")

In the SD, those three key pillars we talked about are all on display. You can see the parabola, the flux of events that are always happening, always changing. You can see how no two events can be exactly alike—there are so many details, etc. And we can never say all there is to say; non-allness at work again, begging the use of the *etc*.

Korzybski originally called the SD an "anthropometer" (measure of man) and the "time-binding differential" (because it showed the difference between humans and other animals). By the time *S&S* came out, he was calling it the "structural differential" and that's the name that stuck.

Korzybski used to build models of the SD out of wood, aluminum discs, violin pegs, and other materials. He even got a lathe to manufacture them at his home. Korzybski spent quite a bit of time and money making these things, of all different sizes, and then gave them away to friends and associates. He got better and better at fashioning them. And some of the later models were apparently quite well made with mahogany wood and gold nibs.

He was a big believer in physically holding the SD and working with it using your hands, to get a real sense for how it worked. I'm fine just looking at it, though I admit it might be cool to have one hanging in my office—a definite conversation piece! Maybe I'll get my son—who studied engineering and is pretty crafty in his workshop—to fashion me one.

There are variations of the SD. I just showed you the classic model here. Some of these variations are quite interesting. I'll get to them in the next letter.

I will also get to what I think is the most important conclusion to draw from the SD.

Your Fellow Time-Binder,

Chris

Letter 8

Variations on the SD

Dear Fellow Time-Binder,

I suppose you're right; the SD does look like abstract art made from junk. Or perhaps we could put a plant in the parabola and turn it into some kind of macrame rope plant hanger—the kind I used to see at my grandmother's house.

Korzybski's SD inspired a number of creative variations, though nobody has made a macrame out of it to my knowledge. I have two favorites that I think are worth sharing for the different points they make.

The original SD, after all, has limitations. It's a model, or abstraction, itself. So it is not a literal representation of what's going on. These variations try to bring in something important that the simpler model does not explicitly show.

Gad Horowitz, whom I mentioned before as the author of *The Book of Radical General Semantics*, talked about one interesting variation devised by one of his students. This SD model—an actual physical model—starts with the parabola as a kind of cloth bag from which the object level, description level, etc., all hang. What's neat here is that they can all be put in the bag.

Horowitz describes it this way:

> I had been emphasizing to the students that although these levels are separate in space in the structural differential, as it is commonly represented, in fact the levels are not separate... The event level contains the object level, even though the object is abstracted from the event. And although the label levels are abstracted from the object level, the object contains the label levels.

The levels—event, object, description, inference, etc.—all exist together and all inhere in the "event." Pretty creative, I say. And insightful, as it reminds us the different pieces of the abstracting process do not happen in a vacuum, but are drenched in the event itself.

Robert Pula came up with another variation based on a Korzybski variant in *S&S* (Korzybski has several diagrams of the SD in *S&S*, each slightly different from the others.) I like Pula's variation because it shows how the abstracting process takes place in space-time and is itself ongoing—thereby correcting any impression by the simpler model that abstracting is a snapshot, a one and done activity. Pula takes several SDs and links them with a large parabola up top:

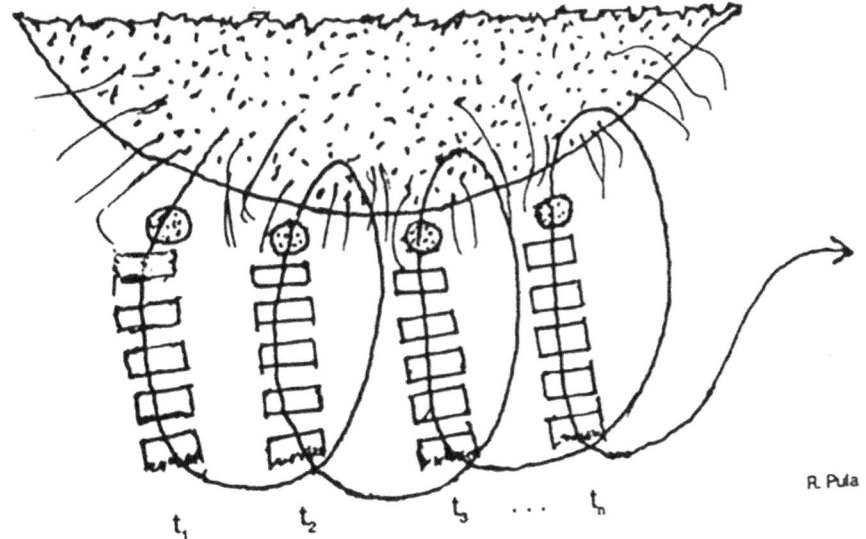

The line with the arrow shows the progression of abstracting over time.

There are more variations, some of which look quite a bit different from the original model. But I think we've covered enough of the basics of the SD for now. Don't worry if you don't entirely get the SD at this point. The more you play with it and use GS, the more you'll "see" and the richer the model becomes.

Korzybski placed a good deal of importance on the SD. He dedicated about a fifth of S&S to discussing the relationship of the SD to the rest of GS. As he writes: "This diagram, indeed, involved all the psychophysiological factors necessary for the transition from the old semantic reactions [evaluations] to the new, and it gives in a way a *structural summary* of the whole non-aristotelian system." (I know, what's a "non-aristotelian system"? We'll get to it. For now, know that GS is one.)

And lest I forget: I wrote in my last letter that I would share the most important conclusion of the SD with you. So here it is: Whatever you say about an object is not the object itself. Whatever descriptions we create are not what we are trying to describe. Or as Korzybski more memorably put it: "*The word is not the thing.*"

The phrase has become one of those touchstones in GS circles, oft-repeated. Korzybski liked to say such a conclusion enjoyed "unusual security" because it was impossible to refute. "If we start, for instance, with a statement that 'a word is *not* the object spoken about,' and someone tries to deny that, he would have to produce an actual physical object which would *be the word*,—impossible of performance, even in asylums. . ."

I love that last bit. Korzybski had a sense of humor. Anyway, the seeming irrefutability of this statement made Korzybski, as a friend of his said, "blasphemously cheerful."

"Whatever we may say will not be the objective level, which remains fundamentally un-speakable," Korzybski wrote. "Thus, we can sit on the object called 'a chair', but we cannot sit on the noise we made or the name we applied to that object."

Baby stuff, right? Nobody goes around believing the word chair is the same thing as the chair itself. Ah, but they do. Maybe not a chair, but think of other descriptions.

There is a funny story that circulates in GS circles about how Korzybski once started eating cookies from a bag in front of his students. He offered to share them. Some students took a cookie and started crunching away. Apparently all was fine. Then Korzybski told them they were eating dog treats. As you can imagine, this changed things. Some students spit them out, etc. But why? Maybe because they let the words be the thing.

I don't know if Korzybski actually gave his students dog treats or not. But what would make the story even better is if he told them they were dog treats, but then, after getting the predictable reaction, showed them a box where they came from—which shows the "cookies" were actually cookies made for human consumption after all.

The word is not the thing. Whatever you say about "it," is not it. We're always *abstracting*, as the SD, in its various glorious variations, reminds us.

This leads to another one of Korzybski's favorite phrases, perhaps his most famous: "the map is not the territory." I'll tell you about it in my next letter.

Your Fellow Time-Binder,

Chris

Letter 9

The Map Is Not the Territory

Dear Fellow Time-Binder,

I'm happy you've heard the phrase: "The map is not the territory." Alan Watts had a version which gets at the same idea, "the menu is not the meal."

What does it mean? I think you'll find it means more than you thought.

Building on what we know from previous letters on the SD, which is itself a representation of map-territory relations, we could say a map is a description, a higher-level abstraction, which leaves things out. The perfect map would have to be a scale version of the territory—and it would have to include a map of the map. On this last point, we'd say the map is "self-reflexive" (we can make maps of maps).

So, an important point about maps is that they can lead us astray. GS books usually explain this idea using a simple map. Something like this:

Chicago — San Francisco — New York

And you say, "Well, there is an obvious problem with this map. San Francisco is not between Chicago and New York. This map is wrong."

Yes, but why do you say it is wrong? Because the map does not fit the territory it describes. In GS, we say the map is not "similar in structure" to the territory it aims to describe. "Similar in structure" is a key phrase in GS, which we will abbreviate to "SiS."

So now, putting these two things together we get an important conclusion. As Korzybski has it: "If words are not things, or maps are not the actual territory, then, obviously, the only possible link between the objective world and the linguistic world is found in structure, and structure alone." (I don't love the adjective "objective" here, which implies there is something permanent that is obvious to everyone. Instead, I would prefer to just say the "world of experience" or the "nonverbal world.")

Our language is a kind of map. Words, ideas, theories, etc. . . all maps. What Korzybski is teaching us here is that our maps are useful insofar as they are SiS to what they try to describe. Korzybski didn't want us to think of the map as being "wrong" or "bad." Because, after all, what does it mean to say a map is "wrong" or "bad"? It sounds like a moral judgment and it doesn't really tell us anything useful about the map's shortcomings. Korzybski wanted to think in terms of structure.

There is an issue with the map example I feel I should address: Nobody will use a map that shows Chicago west of San Francisco because everybody knows where San Francisco is relative to Chicago! If mapmaking were as easy as this, we wouldn't need general semantics. In real life, we often can't check our maps like this. The territory is not knowable in that way; our descriptions represent a lot more guesswork. (And even the simple map above might be right. We really don't have enough information to know. What if the "map" represented a commercial flight? It starts in Chicago, flies to San Francisco and then on to New York?)

The simple example makes a point, but in the world of our experience, all we have are maps. We can't know the territory and check our maps so easily. It is perhaps better to say that GS aims to help people create better maps. Not one that is "right" but one that is "better"—in the sense that is more useful, explains more things, predicts more things, etc.

Some descriptions are easier to "check." If someone says, "Americans want free healthcare," we can readily falsify that map by finding people who fit in the category of "American" and don't want "free healthcare." The index is useful here, too: American$_1$ is not American$_2$. If someone says "Alan Watts was an Episcopal priest," we can improve that "map" by adding a date "up until 1950" when he resigned his ministry.

But if someone says, "Thomas Hobbes did not believe in God," such a map is not something we can verify. There is textual evidence in what he wrote and said, but there is conflicting evidence, and scholars debate the point, with some saying he was a closet atheist and others saying he was basically a sincere Anglican. We'll never know what he "really" thought.

Lots of maps we encounter in our daily life are more like this statement about Hobbes. Think about maps offered by politicians, preachers, movie reviewers, auto mechanics, salespeople, friends, advice columnists, etc. Checking to see if they are SiS to what they aim to describe may be difficult.

So, I think we should keep in mind that when we talk about SiS, we mean "SiS as best we can tell." Thinking this way leaves open the possibility that maps (ours and those of other people) are always subject to improvement. Otherwise, we risk falling in love with our maps, thinking they are "correct" or "true" and, thus, taking them for granted.

We are not powerless to make critiques and improve our maps. GS gives us lots of tools to do that, as you've seen—and there are many more tools I have yet to share.

In addition to SiS, another term you'll come across in the GS literature is "false to facts." So, we could say that the map with Chicago west of San Francisco is "false to facts." In GS, though, we have a high bar for what we'll call a fact.

For a discussion of facts, I want to introduce one of the great teachers of GS, a student of Korzybski's, named Irving Lee. We'll get to him in our next letter.

Your Fellow Time-Binder,

Chris

P.S. "Maps are liars." This pithy line comes from Edmund Carpenter's book *Oh, What a Blow That Phantom Gave Me!* Carpenter writes about Prince Modupe, who grew up in a small village in French Guinea. Modupe once took a map of the Niger River back to his village to give to his father, who had never seen such maps before.

His father was not as impressed as he was and gave his line about maps being liars. The map didn't show depths of waterways, crucial information in crossing them. Distances in miles meant nothing to him, rooted in the experience of actually traveling such distances on foot. In fact, the father seems offended. "I understand now," Prince Modupe wrote, "although I did not at the time, that my airy and easy sweep of map-traced staggering distances belittled the journeys he had measured in tired feet. With my big map-talk, I had effaced the magnitude of his cargo-laden heat-weighted treks."

Prince Modupe's father gives us a memorable example of how maps can be very different from felt experiences and thus, from a certain point of view, not SiS to the territory they aim to describe.

Letter 10
Fact-Finder

Dear Fellow Time-Binder,

Well, Korzybski was fortunate to attract many talented individuals who took up his ideas and helped advance the cause in various ways. While Korzybski is the star, your familiarity with this supporting cast will deepen your understanding of (and appreciation for) GS. Besides, they are engaging figures on their own merits.

With that, let me introduce Irving Lee (1909–1955).

You may remember the name. I mentioned him in an earlier letter, quoting his description of general semantics. Lee wrote a handy book on GS titled *Language Habits in Human Affairs*. I have the original 1941 hardcover edition that I bought at a used bookstore for just four dollars. I don't know that I have ever gotten so much out of four dollars before. *Language Habits* was helpful to me in the early days when I was learning the basics about GS because Lee's language and examples were so clear. Korzybski wrote a laudatory foreword for his former student.

Lee's book is definitely one soaked in the parabola of his times. The events of 1941 cast a shadow over the book. Korzybski talks in his foreword about how "a few sick individuals, through verbal distortions, falsifications, identifications, etc. have trained a whole generation in a pathological use of our *neuro*-semantic and *neuro*-linguistic mechanisms." You can almost feel the old man's blood pressure rising.

For Korzybski, it must've been a sense of déjà vu. He had seen firsthand, in WWI, what horror people could commit in the name of uncritically held abstractions. And here it was happening all over again. The stakes were high, Korzybski always maintained, if we did not correct such abuses. The "sanity of the race" depended on it. "Present-day 'Führers'" have done "endless harm" and we have to take special measures to "prevent the contagious disease of the pathological use of language from being perpetuated." Korzybski's GS is one such special measure.

Lee, too, addressed the war in a 15-page preface. He writes how those who wield power know words can be weapons. These powerful people aim not only to capture territory and supplies, but also to fasten and enchant the minds of people. Lee's preface sounds an ominous tone and has several worthy observations. One thing I'd like to highlight here is his reference to Adolf Hitler, *Mein Kampf*, and Hitler's use of language to persuade people to his way of thinking.

Lee says it's not important to focus on the rhetoric itself but to ask certain questions:

> What is the relationship of what he says to what happens, to the observable life facts which his talk is supposed to represent? How verifiable are his claims? To what extent are his judgments and conclusions manifested as statements of fact? To what degree do his assertions *properly evaluate* with discimination and closeness the world situations about which he talks? These are the questions which the student of General Semantics wants answered.

I like to think that if GS were then more widely known—as common to people's ways of thinking as addition or subtraction—Hitler would never have gotten very far at all. Such a view may be naive, but you must admit falling prey to abstractions can have disastrous consequences.

Lee was born in New York in 1909. His first encounter with GS came in the fall of 1939, when he took one of Korzybski's seminars. At this point, he had just earned his Ph.D. at Northwestern, where he was an instructor in public speaking. Korzybski and GS made a deep impression on him. And in 1940, he began teaching a class "language and thought" inspired by what he had learned. It was a popular class, with as many as 275 students enrolled at one time. The war years interrupted his teaching, and he served in the Air Force from 1942 to 1946, attaining the rank of major.

Lee was, by all accounts, an amazing teacher and a warm, affable human being. He was, also, a great speaker. You can watch him on YouTube. Just search "Irving Lee" and he comes right up. There are six lectures you can watch, part of a series called *Talking Sense*. The first lecture is titled "Just what is General Semantics?" I found them all captivating. Lee is instantly likeable and has an easygoing manner in his way of presenting his material.

Lee died young in 1955. That year, *The General Semantics Bulletin* published over 30 pages of remembrances and appreciations by students and colleagues. The man clearly made an impact.

One of these remembrances by Helen Stevenson recalls the time just before WWII began in earnest for the US. Stevenson's remembrance gets to what was one of Lee's favorite concerns:

Until December 7, 1941, when the United States was drawn into World War II, the Middle West was in the grip of isolationism, anti-Semitism, and pacifism. From Detroit Father Coughlin preached on the radio his own brand of intolerance. Stories of persecution of Jews would leak into the press only to be denied by an "expert" the next day. What a jungle of distortion and what an opportunity to use general semantics! Lee made use of the news, *focusing on the lies and the propaganda to help us sort out statements-of-fact, differences and similarities*. [Italics added].

Sorting out statements-of-fact was something Lee seemed to relish. Martin Maloney, a colleague of Lee's, recalled how he loved to ask the question "What is a fact?" and notes how he took "unfailing delight in the answers and discussions which followed the question."

You can see this trait at work in the *Talking Sense* series, too. At one point, Lee holds up an apple and supposes you say, "there are seeds in this apple." He then asks, is that a statement of fact? Your first reaction is to say "yes." There have been seeds in all the other apples I've dealt with. There must be seeds in this one too.

Then Lee says, "I would like to cast some doubt about that. I would like to ask you to wonder whether that is actually something you know. And if you say this is a statement of fact, I want to ask you to wonder whether you are thinking as carefully as you should... Is it something you can be sure about? Or is it something that seems very, very likely."

Ah, now he's got you thinking...

In GS circles, we like to differentiate between a *fact* and an *inference*. To help sort out what's what, Lee offered some guidance, which I summarize in the table below:

Fact	Inference
You can make a statement of fact after you observe something	You can make anytime
Stays with what can be observed	Goes beyond what can be observed
Is as close to certainty as we can get	Involves degrees of probability

Bob Pula, another important GS teacher, had an even higher hurdle for what he'd call a fact. Pula agreed with Lee but added that the presumed "fact" needed to be public—or verified by another. Private facts are not good enough. Of course, people can err together. There is no guarantee that a "fact" meeting all our tests is something ironclad, or beyond improvement. All our "facts" live with the risk of improvement or rejection.

Most of what we talk about are really inferences. And it's important to note, Lee is not saying we should avoid inferences. That would be impossible. He's saying to raise the bar for what you call a fact and instead appreciate when you're working with inferences.

So, if we get to his example of the apple, we now have an answer to his question. We can take an apple, and we can say it's round; we can talk about its color, or how much it costs, and so on. These are things that can be observed.

But if we say there are seeds in this apple, we go beyond what can be observed. We can't see whether there are seeds in this apple. To do that, we have to cut open the apple. Another way to think about it, Lee offers, is to wonder how certain you are that there are seeds in this apple: "Would you bet your life?" he asks. "I wouldn't. The odds are very great, and it's very probable... but you can't be certain."

I think about Lee anytime I hear the word "fact." For my own purposes, I tend not to use the word "fact" much, except with quotation marks—as kind of a warning that I'm dealing with a concept that may not be a "fact" at all. (We'll get to quotation marks later, another helpful GS device.) When most people say something is a "fact," they are saying they take it for granted. They no longer think about it.

In conversation, I also like to ask people, in a friendly way, "Is that a fact?" For example, I used to own a Chevy Monte Carlo. One time a friend made some comment about how it is an "American made car." I asked him, "Is that a fact?" He looked at me quizzically. Everybody assumes a Chevy is an American made car. But GM workers made this particular car in Canada. And even that is not entirely accurate, as certain parts of the car were manufactured all over the world and came to Canada for final assembly.

You may think it's not important whether or not one goes around thinking Chevies are American made cars. But if you think you don't want to own an American made car and you buy a Toyota, assuming it's made in Japan, when actually it's made in Kentucky... it seems a silly thing to believe and maybe you'd be better off if you spent less on the Chevy.

Besides, popping small abstracting balloons makes it easier to pop bigger balloons later. Think of it as GS calisthenics. If you carry over this kind of thinking when you read history, for example, you will read it in a different way. You find it easier to question all kinds of things and you come to appreciate how there can be widely different narratives about the same "event"—say the American Revolution or the Vietnam War or the events at the US Capitol on January 6, 2021.

Lee's high threshold for facts can lead to some awkward conversations, though, if you're not careful. I remember once when a friend asserted in a casual way, as an accepted fact, that the American Revolution was fought over taxes. I decided to have a little fun and asked, "Is that a fact?" He got a little mad at me. It is easier to believe things we want to believe than hold these most cherished conceptions in doubt. Not that I doubt taxes had a role to play; I'm just saying we only know these things because we've read about them in history books. It's not something we really know, in Lee's sense. Lots of people were involved in the "American Revolution" and it seems more reasonable to think there were many reasons people fought it. GS calisthenics again.

Along these lines, there is a striking tale told in the GS literature about Harry Weinberg. He was teaching a course in GS and trying to get his attendees to understand the difference between facts and inferences. This was in the early 1960s. At one point he asks the class whether the following statement is a fact: "John F. Kennedy is president of the United States."

And of course, they all say "yes!" Weinberg says: "No! We've all been in class for almost an hour. Who's to say as a matter of fact that John Kennedy is president of the United States? It is an inference, although a highly probable one. He might have resigned, his back pain may have incapacitated him, he might even have been killed. Such a statement is not one of fact."

As the story goes, class ended shortly after noon. The date was November 22, 1963. And the students all learned, in a visceral way, what Weinberg meant to teach them. Again, maybe this particular example is not all that consequential. But it makes the point. Sometimes getting mixed up and believing your inferences without question can have serious consequences. ("Suppose the Trojans had checked that wooden horse?" Weinberg asks.) Much of the drama around literature and movies hangs around some kind of faulty inference.

I remember reading a funny story about a Sufi, told by Arthur Osborne in his book *Be Still It Is the Wind That Sings*. Sufis were sometimes known to flout Sharia law, in order to shock people. So the story goes that a Sufi went for a picnic on a riverbank. He's carrying a wine jar and a woman accompanies him. Scandalous! "Orthodox busybodies" decide to investigate what is going on. They find that the wine jar is full of water and the woman is the Sufi's mother. Another faulty inference!

Sanford I. Berman, who was a colleague of Lee's and another GS writer and teacher, tells a funny story about another faulty inference:

> A man, accompanied by a small boy, entered a barber shop, and he asked for a haircut. When the barber had finished with him, the man said, "I'm going next door for a beer while you cut the kid's hair." The

barber gave the boy a haircut and waited for the man to return. Finally, he turned to the kid and asked, "Where in Pete's sake did your father go?"

"Oh," said the boy, "That ain't my father, he's a man who stopped me in the street and asked me if I'd like to get a free haircut."

Berman has a number of good stories about Lee, too. One time Lee was teaching a seminar and said "Give me a directive that I cannot possibly misunderstand." One person said, "Well, write your name on the blackboard." And then Lee went to the blackboard and wrote "your name on the blackboard." As Berman says, it's the easiest thing in the world to misunderstand.

Berman tried the same trick in his own class. He would teach a seminar from 4:30 to 6:00. Then there would be a break for dinner and they would reconvene at 7:00. So, right before the break, Berman lays down his challenge: "You've got one hour during dinner to see if you can think of a directive that I cannot misunderstand."

After dinner the class returns. One guy stood up, and Berman asked him, "OK, what is the directive?" The guy had an eraser in his hand; he threw it at Berman's head and said "Duck."

Berman says, "I did not misunderstand!"

Never let it be said that GS teachers don't have a sense of humor. They seem a jovial bunch to me. And why not? When you realize how much of our world pivots on abstractions, the whole play starts to look rather comical. As Korzybski himself said at his famous 1937 seminar: "A great many of our human troubles are only artificial verbal bubbles, and when they are pricked they burst so there is nothing left but to laugh."

Consider another faulty inference that is widely held as a "fact"—that the sun rises and sets every day. Does it? This one is tougher to sort out because on the surface it seems to be in accord with Lee's three-point checklist for what we'd call a fact. In this case, the error stems more from how we formulate the "fact" using our language than in the event/object we are trying to describe. What we observe nonverbally would be a "fact"—if I were to go outside and point... but technically, the sun does not "rise."

Bucky Fuller, that "affable genie," loved to point out that the Earth orbited the Sun. Therefore, the sun didn't "rise" or "fall." We are standing on Earth and the Earth is a spinning globe. "Up" is only relative to where you are standing at that moment. Things can only fly "in" toward Earth or "out" or "around." There is no "up" and "down." Yes, maybe a technicality, but still fun.

As you can tell, I also enjoy questioning "facts" and gently throwing doubt on widely held convictions. Perhaps that's why I love Lee—and Korzybski and the rest of the merry band. What fun!

You can't check everything of course. When I go to a restaurant, I assume the food is not poisoned. When I get in my car, I assume the tires won't fall off. I sit here typing this in my home office, and I haven't checked to see if the roof won't fall on my head. (Korzybski—per Pula—used to say you're sitting on your assumption. What assumption are you sitting on? That the chair will hold you up!) And just because you determine a description is an inference, doesn't mean it's worthless. Inferences have varying degrees of security—think of Lee's apple example. It's a good bet the apple has seeds in it, but it's not a fact, not something we know.

As with anything in life, you can take GS ideas to ridiculous extremes. I'm not recommending that you do. (Don't bring up the fact that the sun doesn't "set" on a romantic evening!) You'll have to exercise some judgment. But the more you work with these ideas, the more they become second nature.

I'm not saying you won't ever be fooled. Even Korzybski admitted he wasn't always aware of his own abstracting follies. It's a lifetime practice. If the experience of Lee, Korzybski, Berman and others are any indication, then steady application will bring plenty of wisdom, equanimity and unexpected insights.

Your Fellow Time-Binder,

Chris

P.S. By the way, this letter—with its WWII references—reminds me of an interesting term that seems not to have gotten traction in GS circles, but which I like. So, by now, you have the sense of what makes for "good" time-binding— it keeps facts and inferences straight, aims for descriptions that are SiS to what they aim to describe, takes into account the abstracting process represented by the SD, etc.

But clearly "bad" time-binding happens as well—inferences masquerading as fact, maps that are not SiS to the territories they aim to represent, higher-level abstractions disguised as lower-level abstractions, etc. And these can persist over time like a viral strain and manifest in ongoing racist tropes, anti-semitism, blind patriotism, religious bigotry, etc. What can we call this baleful time-binding?

A GS writer named James French came up with the term *crossbind*:

> Bear in mind that in time-binding there may be cross developments that work against the general progressive momentum, just as in a river

there may be crosscurrents that work against the gen-eral flow of the water. I use the term crossbinds to characterize them. Identity theft, for example, would be an example of a crossbind: of something that grew out of record keeping, but that works against it and time-binding in general. . . Another example would be Adolf Hitler's book, Mein Kampf; and then there are certain dogmatic creeds, and so on. A given thing can also have both time-binding and crossbinding elements in play. For example, an automobile can get you across town faster; but the exhaust from cars in general may pollute your lungs. The interplay between time-binding and crossbinding could be said to determine the general rate of progress of the human race.

I like it as a way to talk about time-binding and evaluations that violate GS principles without resorting to those vague judgmental words like *good* and *bad*. Crossbinds are what GS seeks to cure. Even better, GS can inoculate people from being infected by new crossbinds.

Letter 11

What's a Non-Aristotelian System?

Dear Fellow Time-Binder,
    In your last letter, you wrote that it's probably time to explain what Korzybski means by "non-Aristotelian." Let's get to that.

You'll recall the subtitle of Korzybski's great work *S&S: An Introduction to Non-Aristotelian Systems and General Semantics.*

I hardly need to tell you who Aristotle was. Suffice it to say, he is widely regarded as one of the most influential thinkers of all time. The breadth, depth, and complexity of his works are astonishing. I have his complete works, and I have wrestled with them over the years, to little avail, I must admit. I have read his *Nicomachean Ethics* a couple of times, but otherwise my knowledge of the great philosopher is undoubtedly shallow.

Even so, I think it fair to say that Aristotle himself would not be an Aristotelian (in the same way that it is often said Marx was not a Marxist, nor Keynes a Keynesian). Followers have a way of making ideas their own and fidelity to the original ideas become fuzzy over time, as with a copy of a copy of a copy, etc.

So, "Aristotelian" in the sense we're going to use it, does not necessarily impugn the great philosopher himself. A reader of *ETC*, a professor named Thomas Eliot, once suggested that it was the followers of Aristotle "such as Aquinas" who abused his thought and so he recommended we say "non-GS" instead of "Non-Aristotelian."

Korzybski himself actually responded to this letter and defended his choice of non-Aristotelian, or non-A, as historically and etymologically correct. There are three great systems, Korzybski wrote, "synthesized originally by Aristotle, Euclid, and Newton, and so they should be called by their names."

Ergo, an "Aristotelian" orientation is what remains firmly embedded in our culture. It is built on certain assumptions, as Lance State writes: "These assumptions include the notion that a thing is what it is, permanent and unchanging, and that it is always and everywhere the same, that things can always be evaluated in terms of binary oppositions, either/or categories, so that there are no ambiguities, no gray areas or middle ground, that relationships are static and things are discrete and contained, rather than part of a process."

In GS circles, you'll often see Aristotelian logic distilled to three main principles. We could put these three in a table side-by-side to highlight key differences with a non-Aristotelian orientation, as Korzybski saw it:

Aristotelian	Non-Aristotelian
A is A (Law of identity)	A is not A (The map is not the territory)
A is either A or not A (Law of the excluded middle)	A is not all of A (Non-Allness—the map cannot cover all of the territory)
A cannot be both A and not A (Law of Noncontradiction)	A is self-reflexive (A map can be a map of a map)

There is nothing wrong with Aristotelian statements as logical statements. In certain circumstances, they are essential to talk sense. As Wendell Johnson put it, to flatly deny them without qualification would make you an interesting case for a psychiatrist! These propositions represent "truth by convention"; they are true because we say so. That's the way we've set up the game.

Trouble comes when we try to apply them to the messy nonverbal world, when we forget that the verbal constructions are not SiS with what they aim to represent. So while it is true that two equals two, it isn't true to say that two apples are the same as any other two apples, which Aristotelian logic implies. That's why Korzybski viewed Aristotelian logic as a special case. In the process world we seem to live in, a non-A orientation is more congruent with our experiences.

Thus, the Law of Identity dictates that "an apple is an apple." But in GS, we are mindful that the word (or map) "apple" is not, in fact, the thing I am holding in my hand that we call an "apple."

An example of the Law of the Excluded Middle would be thinking that "an apple is either an apple or it is not." In GS, we emphasize the limitations of either/or thinking. There are many varieties of apples with meaningful differences among them and there are gray areas about what is what. We say such labels (maps) cannot capture everything. The term of art in GS is "non-allness."

It may be easier to see it if we try different words. If we say a person is either a genius or not a genius (an example given by Wendell Johnson), we can readily see how such a statement is problematic. Who, exactly, qualifies as a genius? And is that really the way to divide human beings sensibly? It doesn't seem useful or make much sense when viewed through a GS lens.

But we do this kind of thing all the time when we talk about "Republicans" and "Democrats," or "Business" and "Government" or "Farmers" or "Labor" or "Taxpayers" etc. etc.... All blowing verbal bubbles. Another example would be the statement "you either like pizza or you don't." But someone could both like pizza of a certain kind and not like pizza of a different sort.

So, verbal bubbles can get you into trouble, yet we often rely on the validity of reasoning on such categories. A classic example given as a sort of proof of concept is the following:

All men are mortal
Socrates is a man
Therefore, Socrates is mortal

Seems pretty secure, doesn't it? Now consider this one:

All politicians are liars
This man is a politician
Therefore, this man is a liar

Not so secure. In fact, it raises a lot of questions. What makes a politician a liar? And does this mean they lie all the time? Aren't there easy ways to disprove this logic? What if we ask a "politician" a question that he answers with something we can corroborate? And so on...

(By the way, even the Socrates syllogism is not 100% secure. If we want to be technical about it, the validity seems to hinge on what we mean by "mortal." In some ways, you could argue Socrates is practically immortal, forever living on in our literature and imagination. I'm also reminded of how Heinz von Foerster rewrote this syllogism: If all men are mortal and Socrates is a man, then Socrates *may be* mortal. "Look what has happened," von Foerster wrote. "Something has disappeared. It's called certainty!")

And finally the Law of Noncontradiction. An apple cannot be both an apple and not an apple. In GS, we might modify this by saying that something should not be classified as both A and not A in the same context at the same time. To shift the example to make this distinction clear, think of the statement "A college student cannot be both a college student and not a college student." But this statement ignores time and place. A person could be a college student on Monday at 10 a.m., but a grocery clerk on Saturdays between the hours of 9 and 5.

Though not directly related to the Law of Noncontradiction, we round out the table by including a key GS principle: All of our descriptions (or maps) are self-reflective—that is, we can make maps of our maps and so on.

Before we leave these three propositions, I want to emphasize again: the problem is not with logic, the problem comes when we use it unthinkingly in the world of experience. As Johnson put it, "it is easier to be logical than it is to be sensible." Anybody can set up definitions and then make logical statements using the propositions on the left-hand side of the table. But that doesn't mean that they have made any sense.

For example, a friend of mine likes to rant about "postmodernists" and "postmodernism"—categories he picked up from a YouTube "intellectual," and based on which he assigns various beliefs and makes various deductions. His bugbear, though, is a fiction, a work of imagination. Nothing in our world of experience answers to his categories. Yet, he continues to wage political war against this unseen enemy. "In logic lurks wizardry" in Johnson's marvelous phrase. Indeed, it can make people believe and do nutty things.

In *S&S*, Korzybski has a table that runs over three pages and highlights 52 points of difference between an Aristotelian orientation and a non-Aristotelian orientation. But my task here is not to delineate all the differences, which could be a book in itself. I merely want you to have some understanding of why Korzybski called his system a "non-Aristotelian" one.

There are two other important points to make here.

First, Korzybski is an admirer of Aristotle's and includes him in the dedication of *S&S*. Too often, people incorrectly assume "non-Aristotelian" means "anti-Aristotelian." Not so. But Korzybski thought of non-Aristotelian thought as more advanced—in the sense that it can explain more things and is more in line with modern science—than Aristotelian logic.

A similar analogy holds with Euclid's geometry and subsequent non-Euclidean geometries (i.e, Lobachevsky), and Newton's physics and non-Newtonian physics (such as Einstein's or Quantum Physics). These "non-" systems came about and destroyed an old absolute. Not *the* geometry of 'space', but *a* geometry. Not *the* universe of Newton, but *a* universe among other interpretive possibilities. The same with non-Aristotelian thought...

Which brings me to the second important point: GS is *a* non-Aristotelian system. There are others. Here are some examples:

> Wittgenstein's Philosophy of Language
> Kurt Gödel's Incompleteness Theorem
> Edward Sapir and Benjamin Whorf's Linguistic Relativism
> Albert Einstein's Theory of Relativity
> Werner Heisenberg's Uncertainty Principle

gNorbert Wiener's Cybernetics
Gregory Bateson's Ecology of Mind
Paul Watzlawick's Relational Communication
George Lakoff and Mark Johnson's Metaphor Theory
Marshall McLuhan and Neil Postman's Media Ecology

Norbert Wiener's name brings to mind a funny story told by Stafford Beer.

The story goes that the Wiener family moved to a house not far from their old one. Norbert could be extremely forgetful about such things—the epitome of the "absent-minded professor." So on the last day in his old house, his wife reminded him when he came home from work that he needed to walk to the new address, down the street.

Despite this reminder, Norbert goes to his old home at the end of the day and sees it is dark and then remembers. "Ah, we moved." But he forgets where, though he knows it's close by. He sees a little girl playing in the street and asks if she knows where the Wieners had gone. She replies, "Of course I do, Daddy!"

Your Fellow Time-Binder,

Chris

P.S. Aristotle's teachings dominated intellectual life and even became part of the dogma of the Church. At times and in certain places, the effect was incredibly stifling. For example, in Paris in 1624, there was a decree that forbade attacks on Aristotle. The penalty of disobedience was death.

Pushback to Aristotle's dominance began with two important philosophers: Francis Bacon (1561–1626) and René Descartes (1596–1650). I would like to share several points about these thinkers, especially Bacon, whose concerns echo in Korzybski's work.

Bacon often marks the beginning of modern philosophy. If you read a history of philosophy, he's usually the first modern, coming right after the Renaissance. John Dewey, in his *Reconstruction in Philosophy*, called Bacon "the real founder of modern thought." And scholar Perez Zagorin wrote that you could "helpfully regard [Bacon's project] as an extended attack upon... the old regime of knowledge." (Bacon seemed to be a difficult person. Hobbes' biographer A.P. Martinich wrote "Not even his friends liked him.")

Bacon called his magnum opus *The New Organum*, which implicitly reveals its aim to replace Aristotle's *Organum*. *The New Organum* is not a long work and is surprisingly readable in modern editions. (I read the Hackett edition edited by Rose-Mary Sargent.)

There are passages in *The New Organum* that sound very much like something Korzybski would say. For example, Bacon warns against putting too much stock in propositions, which "consist of words, words are symbols of notions. Therefore if the notions themselves... are confused and overhastily abstracted from the facts, there can be no firmness in superstructure."

He complains of ill-defined, abstract words, such as "essence," "quality," "passion," "rare," "corruption," "element," and "form." "All are fantastical and ill-defined," Bacon writes. This is also something Korzybski writes about—over/under defined terms—which I will leave for a future letter.

One of Bacon's most famous formulations is his "idols of mind," which give us four origins for error and misconceptions. Korzybski approved of these, writing in *Manhood of Humanity*, "the idols and medieval fetishes which he so masterfully describes are equally venerated today." Korzybski goes on to quote six passages from *The New Organum* about the idols, running over three pages in the book.

The first idols are *idols of the tribe* and include limitations built into our nervous systems, or, as he says "perceptions." These are common to all humankind.

Next came *idols of the cave*, which include misconceptions that stem from our own individual biases and preferences. We all live in our caves, so to speak, which give us a unique perspective.

Idols of the marketplace are errors we inherit from mixing with others and using language, where "ill and unfit choice of words wonderfully obstructs the understanding" and "throw all into confusion, and lead men away into numberless empty controversies and idle fancies."

And finally, *Idols of the theater* come from the false "dogmas of philosophies" and false demonstrations, which Bacon likens to the fictions of the theater.

In a sense, GS is a project that aims to make one aware of these idols and offer ways to correct and cope with them. Bacon, too, saw that names did not match up with what they aim to describe and that they could give "substance and reality to things which are fleeting." We "name things which do not exist." We can become the "slave of words."

Bacon urges close attention to particulars and encourages experiments. He warns against blindly accepting "the authority of men accounted great... by general consent." He decries superstition and "immoderate zeal of religion" as stumbling blocks to greater understanding. Bacon is suspicious of those who would spin ideas out their heads without regard to testing their findings against the empirical world.

A Baconian person is one who marries experiment *and* reason. Bacon includes a poetic metaphor in *The New Organum*, in which he likens his ideal thinking person to a bee: "The men of experiment are like the ant; they only collect and use. The reasoners resemble spiders, who make cobwebs out of their own substance. But the bee takes the middle course. It gathers material from the flowers of the gardens and of the field, but transforms and digests it by a power of its own."

Like Korzybski, Bacon sought to provide tools to make us aware of our limitations, our abstracting and to bring our evaluations more in line with what is going on. "For I do not take away the authority of the senses," Bacon wrote, "but supply them with helps." Korzybski's working devices are akin to Bacon's "helps."

Briefly, let's turn to Descartes. He came out against Aristotle from a different direction, but again is quite explicit in his target. In a letter to his friend Mersenne, Descartes writes that he hopes those who read his principles "will recognize the truth before noticing that they destroy those of Aristotle."

As with Bacon's œuvre, Descartes' chief works, *The Discourse on Method* and *Meditations on First Philosophy*, are not long and quite readable. (I recommend the Hackett edition, edited by Roger Ariew.) And as with Bacon, Descartes declares his great break from the old authorities. Descartes pledged he will search for no knowledge "other than what could be found within myself, or else in the great book of the world" i.e., experience. "I learned not to believe anything too firmly of which I had been persuaded only by example and custom" and thus he freed himself from the baggage of the past and stifling influence of accepted authority. Cartesian doubt challenged the truthfulness of the senses, of observations—directly contrary to Aristotelian thinking.

Descartes' influence was immense. Richard Watson, in his biography of Descartes, argues that he "laid the foundation for the dominance of reason in science and human affairs."

Descartes comes into the GS story again later in an important way. Korzybski, in *Manhood*, praises Descartes' work—along with those of Newton and Leibniz—for discoveries in *mathematics*. But he would forcefully reject one of Descartes' main contributions to philosophy. ("Elementalism" is the key word here, and we'll tackle it in a future letter.) For now, let us simply appreciate the bold revolution Bacon and Descartes set off. Neither could totally escape the old ways of thinking—perhaps as expected of pioneers. Later thinkers would continue to push these ideas forward.

Korzybski would be one of them—another voice in a line that began with (especially) Bacon and Descartes. Kendig thought so too, and she saw *S&S* as completing a trilogy that began with Aristotle's *Organum* and Bacon's *New Organum*.

Letter 12

Alfred Korzybski after *Science & Sanity*

Dear Fellow Time-Binder,
    As to the impact of Korzybski's book *Science & Sanity*, I suppose it depends. To answer you, I think it worthwhile to fill in a little more historical background on the book and our man Korzybski.

S&S came out in 1933, amidst the Great Depression. Charlotte Schuchardt Read, a long-time close associate of Korzybski's, recalled the $7 price tag of the book "seemed astronomical." "Even the special price of $5.50 for teachers in those days was probably very hard for most to meet," she wrote. (Read studied with Korzybski in 1936 and became his editorial secretary in 1939. She wore many hats for GS causes until her death in 2002 at the age of 92.)

Nonetheless, the book garnered positive reviews and sold well enough—about 2,500 copies in its first year. Enough to undergo a second edition in 1941, with a new 50-page introduction. Sales of *S&S* increased steadily in the 1940s, hitting a high of 3,200 copies in 1949. There would be a third edition in 1948 and fourth in 1958 (the first edition that Korzybski himself would not oversee, since he died in 1950). *S&S* remains in print today, in a handsome 5th edition.

As for influence, it is hard to say. Certainly, the book had an impact on a wide range of thinkers. Some thought it a very important book. Anatol Rapoport wrote that "[Korzybski] was the precursor of an intellectual revolution unequalled since the renaissance." Hyperbolic, probably, but the book did inspire many other books, papers, essays, speeches, etc. As I said, it's hard to measure influence. (Rapoport was a fascinating character himself and an important GS teacher. I'll have to introduce you to him in a future letter.)

Still, we can map out some of the interesting things that happened after *S&S* came out. Korzybski worked hard on the book, incorporating a vast reading that stretched across many disciplines. The first edition lists 619 books in the bibliography. W. Benton Harrison, a GS writer and former student of Korzybski's, recalls asking Korzybski once if he actually read all the books in the bibliography. "With a quick look of surprise and even scorn," Harrison recalls, "[Korzybski] replied 'Certainly—and studied all of them and many articles not included!'"

Twelve years in the making, *S&S* is quite an achievement. It can seem an intimidating book—over 800 pages in relatively small print, with some math (especially in Book III), unfamiliar vocabulary ("structural differential," etc.) and quirky punctuation (those devices!) mixed in. Some dubbed it "the blue peril," as the original edition had a blue cover (as the 5th edition does today). Nonetheless, I can attest *S&S* repays study and re-reading.

I'll admit, I got stuck on my first attempt. Yet, I knew there were important ideas in this book that I wanted to understand. I didn't give up so easily. I read Korzybski's Olivet College lectures, which was a simpler presentation of GS ideas. And with the aid of *Pula's Guide for the Perplexed*, I did read *S&S* through on the second attempt. It has been a life-changing book for me. And I greatly value the insights Korzybski shared. I hope these letters will inspire you in a similar way to study GS.

Korzybski was a busy man after the book's publication. Martin Levinson, a long-time scholar in general semantics and former president of the Institute of General Semantics, wrote that *S&S* "created a major stir among scholars and intellectuals." Read reports that Korzybski began to travel around America to promote his book. Between January 1935 and July 1938, Korzybski gave seminars or lectures at a dozen colleges and universities, three hospitals and two conferences in St. Louis and Los Angeles. (Read wrote a piece titled "The Institute of General Semantics: A Brief Historical Survey," from which I draw most of these historical notes.)

In 1938, Korzybski established the Institute of General Semantics (IGS) in Chicago, thanks to the initial funding of $25,000 by Cornelius Crane (heir to the Crane Plumbing fortune). Korzybski invited scholars, many of whom he corresponded with in researching *S&S*, to join as honorary trustees. Thirty-one accepted.

Korzybksi also began giving seminars at the Institute, which eventually settled in a house with the memorable address of 1234 E. 56th street. Many of the future leaders of GS came to these seminars, including Irving Lee, Wendell Johnson, Francis Chisholm, and S.I. Hayakawa (more on him in another letter).

Some of the more famous personalities that came to seminars and workshops included William S. Burroughs, Buckminster Fuller, sci-fi writer Robert Heinlein, the psychologist Abraham Maslow, the entertainer Steve Allen, and author Robert Anton Wilson (or RAW, as he is known to his fans).

In fact, reading RAW introduced me to GS and Korzybski. He often mentioned Korzybski and GS in his nonfiction books. Then I read a transcript of a lecture RAW gave where he said he learned more from Korzybski than any other writer. That endorsement was enough to make me research Korzybski, who I did not know at the time. I've been hooked ever since.

The heyday for GS was probably in the 1940s. It was around this time that the first "popularizations" began to appear: *The Tyranny of Words* (1938) by Stuart Chase, *Language in Action* (1941) by S. I. Hayakawa, *Language Habits in Human Affairs* (1941) by Irving Lee, and *People in Quandaries* (1946) by Wendell Johnson. These were among the most famous and most enduring. Hayakawa's book especially, which became a Book-of-the-Month selection and sold millions of copies, introduced GS to a broad audience.

Korzybski's IGS was an ambitious project, with frequent seminars and publications, though often scrambling for funding. In 1946, IGS moved to Lakeville, Connecticut. And then on to Lime Rock, CT, in an old house bought by Kendig—"French Second Empire style" Read tells us—where it would reside until 1983. "It was a major challenge for the Institute staff to adjust to functioning in the country," Read wrote, "ninety miles from New York and many miles from a town of more than 2,000. Five miles from Lakeville, and too small to have a post office able to handle our mail, Lime Rock was a 'ghost town' in 1946."

Other societies for GS popped up, too. In 1946, in Chicago, Korzybski students established the Society for General Semantics. This became the International Society for General Semantics, or ISGS, an important group that started the *ETC: A Review of General Semantics* in 1943 with Hayakawa as editor. ISGS merged with IGS in 2003. Other societies emerged in New York, Montreal, Los Angeles, San Francisco, and Ann Arbor. And up to a hundred colleges and universities offered courses in GS. Read says in the years 1947–50, seminars were so full that the Institute couldn't hold them on site because they lacked space.

Korzybski seemed a tireless worker. Keeping his small institute afloat took tremendous personal effort, as well as help from his able associates. He seemed to work constantly. W. Benton Harrison wrote that Korzybski often gave two 3-hour lectures a day. Harrison includes a delightful description of Korzybski worth quoting at length here:

> Physically, Korzybski was 5 feet 8 or 9 inches tall, weighed about 165 pounds, was of a stocky build and powerful of body and voice... Nearly always he wore clean and neatly pressed trousers and a shirt open at the collar, and on only a few occasions were his associates able to persuade him to wear a jacket. Some thought him gruff and curt because he was usually serious and was not given to small talk, but he often gave evidence of a well developed sense of humor.
>
> He demanded little of life in the way of comforts or luxuries. He wanted and collected a sizable and interesting library. I never saw him

take more than two drinks (always rum), despite some of the stories I have heard. His bearing and force of personality seemed to have a special appeal to the ladies in a "Yul Brynner" manner; at least he was equally bald.

Harrison also reports Koryzbksi's booming voice required no microphones and that he spoke with a "slight accent (*neurosis* was 'new roses')." In his lectures, he'd often use "props." Harrison recalls one involving a penny box of matches. When shaken, it made no sound, and students would conclude it was empty. Then Korzybski would open the box and show it was "too full to rattle." This would be an opening to speak about reliance on unconscious inferences and untested assumptions.

By 1949, things seemed to be going pretty well for the old Count. Korzybski gave a seminar at Yale, where a number of professors participated. Sales of *S&S* were hitting peaks. Korzybski was working on a second edition of *Manhood of Humanity*. And GS seemed to be gaining traction in the public discourse. But the end was near for Korzybski.

In April 1950, he was invited to speak at a symposium at the University of Texas. He had nearly finished his paper when, in the early morning of March 1, Korzybski died suddenly of a heart attack.

Kendig, who became the Director of IGS, wound up delivering his last paper, "The Role of Language in the Perceptual Process," at the University of Texas. And Dr. J. Samuel Bois delivered the August seminars, the first without Korzybski.

GS would go on without its founder. And the framework he created would endure. *S&S* remains in print today and as relevant as ever. Korzybski's magnum opus swells with great ambition and yet there is an underlying modesty to the project. Korzybski often acknowledges his own limitations, his expectation that some of what he writes may be proven wrong later and even exceeded by the work of others. GS, after all, teaches epistemological modesty. (Pula would call it "epistemodesty.") Korzybski knew he could never say all that was to be said.

Korzybski peppered the book with a lot of quotes from scientists, philosophers, and other thinkers, past and present. He justified this by saying he wanted to show that the ideas he wrote about were out there. His great contribution was to systematize them under one roof, called GS.

Not everyone reacted positively to such a strong, eccentric personality, as you might expect.

But based on my reading, I am inclined to agree with his biographer, Bruce Kodish: "I have come to see him as a remarkably kind and well-balanced person, despite some hard edges and personal foibles."

So, that completes a thumbnail sketch of Korzybski, the influence of *S&S*, and the IGS. But the story is hardly complete. *S&S* is a book rich in ideas and provocations. So there's more GS to explore yet. I think it's a good time to introduce you to Korzybski's "safety devices."

Your Fellow Time-Binder,

Chris

Letter 13

Safety Devices

Dear Fellow Time-Binder,

So, you remember we mentioned Descartes? The French philosopher famously declared, "I think, therefore I am." And he gave us one of our most enduring dualisms—the "mind" and the "body." This distinction did not start with Descartes. (You can find it in Plato, for example.) But it takes its modern form in Descartes and people most often associate the idea with him.

In GS, we push back on this dualism. Instead, we say that mind and body are linguistic categories only. We do not find them split like this in the empirical world. Have you ever come across a "mind" without a "body"? Or a "body" without a "mind"? (No wisecracks!)

We call splitting events that are not split in the world "out there" *elementalistic* (or *el*) thinking. Instead, we aim for *non-elementalistic* (or *non-el*) thinking. This is where we use Korzybski's "safety devices," of which there are two: quotation marks and the hyphen.

For any problematic terms, we use a single-quotation mark, like so: 'mind' and 'body.' We may say 'mind' but the quotation mark reminds us that the term 'mind' should be handled with care. Preferably, we would use a hyphen and say mind-body. This brings the two concepts together, properly emphasizing their non-el character.

A great deal of Western philosophy would dissolve if denied this dualism of 'mind' and 'body.' And we might know more about ourselves as well. Rollo May, in his study of anxiety, points out that there has been plenty of research in isolated areas of neurology or physiology about anxiety, and even apparent breakthroughs. But they always disappoint because anxiety is not found in isolation. We need to think about the organism as a whole. May writes, in what could have come out of the pages of Korzybski, "we need to move toward an integrated theory of mind-body." (May, by the way, had some familiarity with Korzybski's work.)

Another famous dualism is 'space' and 'time.' Can we actually split 'space' and 'time' empirically? Think about it. There is no 'space' without existing in 'time.' And there is no 'time' without 'space.' Hence, we say space-time. (An ironic side note: If Korzybski wanted to aim for maximum consistency, he should've called human beings "space-time-binders.")

Using single quotes this way is not standard practice. And it extends beyond just el thinking. You can use quotation marks for any term you deem problematic. As part of their style guide, the *General Semantics Bulletin* used to carry the following note in every issue: "Single quotation marks: To mark off terms and phrases which seem to varying degrees questionable for neuro-linguistic, neurophysiological, methodological or general epistemological reasons, e.g., 'mind', 'meaning', 'space' or 'time' used alone, etc." From here on out, now that you know, I'll be using single quotes in just this way.

Other times I might add a single quotation when I'm talking about a discipline, such as 'philosophy' or 'biology.' The quotation marks remind me that there is no such thing out there called 'philosophy' or 'biology.' As Bucky used to say, nature doesn't have separate departments for 'physics', 'biology', 'mathematics', etc. Nature doesn't need to have a department meeting to know what to do when a leaf drops in the water. 'Philosophy' is what people say it is. And for all but professors and people who run universities, such divisions are not important.

I like to use single quotation marks for many descriptions, because, again, use of such adjectives often raise underlying questions. Something is 'big' 'great' 'small' 'warm' 'cold' etc.... but compared to what?

Getting back to el and non-el thinking: Another example is 'thinking' and 'feeling.' These, again, are linguistic categories. There really is no distinction empirically. So, we prefer to say in GS thinking-feeling—except, I might add, in casual conversation where we see no harm in the distinction.

'Organism' and 'environment' form another classic pair in the GS literature. There is no 'organism' apart from its environment. In GS, we like to say, 'organism-as-a-whole-in-its-environment.' Quite a mouthful, perhaps, but an important idea.

Now, it is possible to make the case that everything is connected to everything else. So any distinction is elementalistic. Thus, one might belittle Korzybski's insight to nothing more than a recommendation against formulating logical impossibilities. Edward MacNeal, a GS teacher and author of a good book title *Mathesemantics*, addressed this concern in an article in *ETC*. He gives us a workable guide to making non-el distinctions: "Whenever one event has no noticeable effect on another event, then we will say that the two events are separate."

So, what you ate for breakfast seems to have no connection to what the stock market does that day. Therefore, we can talk about these events separately without being accused of elementalism. Context matters, too. MacNeal offers the example of a copper mine in Montana and people living in Montana. They are separate events if the question is "how many red-headed people live in Montana?" But are they separate events if the question is "why do people live in Montana?" It would not be elementalistic to separate them in the first example, but it would be in the second.

The basic goal here is to try to improve our *evaluations*. In doing so, we'll improve our time-binding skills. Korzybski's thinking here lines up with classic systems thinkers, such as Heinz von Foerster—who I mentioned in an earlier letter when writing about syllogisms.

Foerster was born in 1911 in Vienna and died in 2002 at the age of 90. He became an important thinker in the field of cybernetics. And he is often included in a group of thinkers labelled "constructivists," which include Ernst von Glassersfeld and others. I think of them as non-Aristotelian thinkers and largely compatible with Korzybsk's project. (I'm vastly simplifying here).

Von Foerster, for example, resisted the way most scientists think of the brain. He insisted the brain functions as part of a whole system, and we should be reluctant ascribing certain qualities to parts of the brain—for example, by saying damage to one part of the brain impedes speech or vision.

He used the analogy of a car. Suppose a mechanic finds there is dirt that is blocking the fuel line and preventing you from starting your car. Would you say that the car's ability to move is localized in the fuel line? "That's ridiculous!" Von Foerster said. "The whole system determines the car's capacity for locomotion." While an injured brain may have constraints, it still functions as part of a whole system. (Rollo May would have agreed.) Here is Von Foerster:

> We must look at the entire system and avoid the temptation to look at one little corner of it or treat it like a machine that can be disassembled so each part can be understood separately. The system must be understood by looking at all the parts together.

What's a system? Well, a system functions as a whole. Meaning, you can't divide a system and expect it to function. Consider an interesting analogy from Draper Kauffman (*Systems One: An Introduction to Systems Thinking*). If you divide a cow in half, that doesn't mean you have two smaller cows. Cows are systems and function as a whole, as a system. Likewise, if you divide a brain in two, you don't get two brains. A brain is a system, part of a broader nervous system, etc., we call a human body.

However, if you take a carton of ice cream and scoop out a cupful, you just have less ice cream. The arrangement of the parts doesn't matter. Systems thinkers call events like cartons of ice cream "heaps." A pile of sand is a heap;

not a system.

Also, there are systems and there are systems within systems. There is the universe made up of galaxies. Galaxies made up of solar systems, and so on like this:

- Universe
- Galaxies
- Solar Systems
- Planets
- Local Ecosystems
- Individual Nervous Systems
- Cells
- Molecules
- Atoms
- Particles

Nested systems within systems. Where you mark the dividing line among systems seems somewhat arbitrary. Nonetheless, systems thinking keeps you aware of "wholes" and helps prevent elementalistic orientations—which, again, are not SiS. Systems thinking is SiS to the way the world seems to behave.

As with all devices, I am not saying you have to be an extremist and start correcting people and making a nuisance of yourself. Safety devices, like their cousins the working devices, work best when used judiciously, not as a knee-jerk reaction. But I think you should strive to use them yourself, if only silently, in your own thinking. That is how they begin to do their work.

The safety devices and the working devices together are called "extensional devices." *Extensional* has an important meaning in GS and contrasts with *intensional*. An extensional orientation means one that looks outward at the empirical world. So, if I ask you "What is a cat?" and you point to a cat, that's an extensional definition. If you gave me a dictionary definition, that's intensional. Korzybski wants us to cultivate an extensional orientation. To appreciate differences, where others see similarities.

Korzybski said using the devices made him 'think' deeper. "That is the art of 'thinking,' because you orient yourself to 'reality' all the time," he wrote, "not in terms of fictitious definitions." This is one of the areas where GS has had the biggest impact on me. Korzybski has opened my eyes as to how so many disagreements come down to definitions. But I will have more to say about this in another letter. For now, let's stay with the safety devices.

With the five extensional devices, you have an important toolkit, or method. Korzybski said that GS was "like another kind of algebra." Just as knowing algebra alone doesn't solve problems, neither does knowing GS. You have to apply the tools to real-world problems.

When you do practice, they really start to change your thinking. I mentioned before how I don't use the word 'fact' without quotation marks. Well, now you know what I was talking about. For me, I try not to use the word 'truth' either. There's just too much baggage in the word. I notice how it tends to promote lazy thinking and allow one to easily slip into dogmatism. If something is 'true,' after all, then you don't need to think about it anymore. But lots of things seemed 'true' at one time and are no longer 'true.' Why not leave yourself open to the possibility that what you think is 'true' at the moment might not always be?

So, I try not to use the word, and if I do I use quotation marks. Or I'll say something like "I suspect that's 'true.'" The word "suspect" in there seems to work wonders. There is a whole host of words I use with care and the quotation marks are a big aid as reminders.

'Good' and 'bad' are another pair of 'opposites' where quotation marks usefully remind us to ask further questions. What is 'good' really? I may say GS is 'good' for you. But I may say more usefully that GS will improve your critical thinking skills (which is still pretty general, but better than just saying 'good.') I might think missing out on a business opportunity is 'bad,' but what does that mean?

On this, I must share the "horse story." I first heard it from Alan Watts. It goes like this: Once upon a time there was a farmer who lost a horse. It ran away. His neighbors told him, "that's too bad." But the farmer replied, "Maybe." The next day the horse returned with seven wild horses. The neighbors say, "That's great!" But the farmer says, "Maybe." The next day the farmer's son tries to break in one of the wild horses. He is thrown and breaks his leg. "That's bad," his neighbors say. But the farmer remains circumspect: "Maybe." The next day officers come to draft young men for a war. And the farmer's son, who has a broken leg, is spared. "Very lucky," say the neighbors. But the farmer says, "Maybe."

The point is: You just never know. A friend of mine and I frequently invoke the horse story when we talk about the events that have 'happened' to us. The horse story keeps you humble. It helps you bear apparent misfortunes with good cheer. It reminds you to be equanimous in the face of apparent successes.

The horse story reveals another aspect to our life in a process world—it's extreme complexity and inherent uncertainty. We'll talk more about GS and uncertainty in a future letter.

In addition to embracing uncertainty, part of being a GS-oriented person, a skilled time-binder, is understanding that we can never exhaust the number and kinds of descriptions and inferences we can make.

Again, we live in a process world, so events are constantly happening. Therefore, we should not expect that descriptions made, say, two thousand years ago should hold up today. Excessive reverence for the descriptions created by our ancestors impedes the creative process and stunts fresh time-binding efforts from emerging.

However, we should not be condescending to our ancestors either. They worked with what ideas they had at the time, building on the time-binding efforts of those that came before them. The best we can say about our circumstances is that we have the ability to talk about more things and do more things and explain more things than our predecessors. This represents progress in a GS sense. We have a richer inventory of descriptions, thanks to the time-binding efforts of those who came before us. If we are successful time-binders, our descendants will inherit a richer inventory of descriptions than we have. And thus, they will be able to talk about more things, do more things, explain more things, than us.

There seems to be no final answer. There is no end 'truth'—so far as we know. The answer to any theory or description or inference is always another theory or description or inference. These later efforts are 'better' not in the sense of being 'truer', but could be 'better' in the GS sense by enriching our inventory of descriptions. Or they could be crossbinds, where they make things 'worse.'

Your Fellow Time-Binder,

Chris

P.S. The classic five extensional devices are the date, the index, etc., the hyphen, and single quotation marks. One GS teacher, Gad Horowitz—you may remember him, author of *The Book of Radical General Semantics*—suggests a sixth: empathy or EM. It works like this: after somebody's name, you put a subscript EM. So, Donald Trump$_{EM}$.

The point of this device is to remind you that if you grew up and had all the experiences and genetic makeup, etc., of Donald Trump, then you'd be Donald Trump. Horowitz says it would be a mistake to dismiss this as a mere tautology. He calls this insight a secularized version of "there but for the grace of God go I," an implication of the chain-index. I want to quote Horowitz here as he lays it out with elegance:

> The individual time-binder's ability to imagine self as-if other is an essential foundation of their cooperation and solidarity with other human beings... It is among humanity's most precious gifts and it can

be improved and enhanced with conscious practice, as with the EM device.

A beautiful sentiment. Who wouldn't welcome a little more empathy in the world? It is also a nice illustration of how creative powers applied to GS can result in a wonderful new device and a new emphasis. Perhaps you can create your own.

Letter 14

English Minus Absolutes

Dear Fellow Time-Binder,

Your intuitions are spot on. GS does tend to eliminate thinking in terms of absolutes. In fact, one GS teacher wrote about what he called "English Minus Absolutes," or EMA.

Allen Walker Read was his name. He was married to Charlotte Schuchardt Read, who we met in previous letters. Both lived to ripe old ages—Allen to 96 and Charlotte to 92. Whereas Charlotte dedicated her professional life to general semantics, Allen was known more for his work outside of GS. Nonetheless, he wrote about two dozen papers on GS and his work remains highly regarded in GS circles.

In fact, both Reads were highly regarded as exemplars, not only in their written work, but in how they conducted themselves as people. Steve Stockdale, a former IGS president, wrote "Allen and Charlotte each served as role models of what Korzybski called the 'extensional orientation.'" And Susan Presby Kodish wrote in a *General Semantics Bulletin*: "Were Abraham Maslow still alive, I'd nominate them for inclusion in his pantheon of self-actualized, fully-human individuals."

So that gives you some idea of the kind of people the Reads were.

Now, to EMA. Allen Walker Read introduced the idea in a paper titled "Language Revision By Deletion of Absolutisms." This simple seven-page paper has influenced me ever since the day I read it.

Read recommends we make certain vocabulary choices to bring our language more in line with the world as we find it. That world, you'll recall, is a process world, a Heraclitean world where we can never step in the same river twice. It is a world where our descriptions are always subject to revision. Thus our evaluations likewise should reflect this changing world and should express probabilities and likelihoods. "Therefore we would do well to avoid finalistic, absolutistic terms," Read writes. "Can we ever find *perfection* or *certainty* or *truth*? No! Then let us stop using such words in our formulations."

Using EMA is not difficult. As Read points, instead of saying "I'm *certain* that. . ." how hard is it to instead say "It *seems to me* that. . ."? I love using "seems." It takes the certainty out. It reminds me that I don't *really* know. I'm communicating the way I see it, the way things seem to me.

Similarly, it's easy to not use, or think carefully before you do use, the words *always* or *never*, or *all* or *same*. Kenneth Keyes, Jr., author of *Taming the Mind*, offers a slew of suggestions here:

"Many" or "most" instead of *all*
"Usually" instead of *always*
"Seldom" instead of *never*
"Similar" instead of *same*

Keyes was a student of Korzybski's and has been described as a documentarian of Korzybski the man. He made a short silent film of Korzybski, which took place in 1944 at the Institute of General Semantics in Chicago, Illinois, and in 1947 in Warm Springs, Georgia. You remember the picture of Korzybski I shared in an earlier letter? Keyes took it.

Keyes (pronounced "Kize") offers other helpful phrases to use to avoid absolutist thinking. They are:

- *up to a point* (or *"to a degree"* or *"to an extent"*)
- *so far as I know*
- *to me*

These are simple to use. Instead of saying, "Reading this book will make you smarter" add "to a degree." Instead of saying, "Margaret doesn't like to go to the beach," we can add "so far as I know." Instead of "It's a long drive" add "to me."

You'll notice that using Korzybski's other devices help do the work for you on this front as well. For example, "Margaret$_{2019}$ doesn't like to go to the beach"—but she might now! So to some extent, these efforts are duplicative. You can choose what works best for you, but I think it is good to know both ways. Often, I feel it is easier to pick out absolutist language than it is to pick up on situations where one should use, say, the date or index.

In any case, each of Keyes' phrases perform a certain function in shifting the way you think.

Adding *up to a point*, or *to a degree*, fights the urge to make things black or white: Is government bureaucracy inefficient? Are pharma executives greedy? (Note you could use the index here—pharma executives$_x$, as they are not all exactly alike!) Is your neighbor a jerk? Well, maybe up to a point. . .

Adding *so far as I know* keeps some sense of humility about what you really know. Is the road clear? Is the car full of gas? *So far as I know.*

Adding *to me*, keeps in mind that you have a point of view, but it is not the only point of view. Obama or Bush was a 'poor' president. . . . *to me*. Shakespeare is boring *to me*. The small addition seems to instantly defuse provocative statements. Others will surely disagree, but, as Keyes said, perhaps the disagreements will be less disagreeable. The "to me" seems to grant instant legitimacy to opposing views.

Both Keyes and Read recognize that we use absolutist terms in lots of situations that do not cause any harm. Watching a ballgame, we might say "So-and-so never strikes out!" Of course, we don't mean it literally. Or when we express gratitude for a gift and say "It's perfect!" Again, we don't literally mean it's perfect. We are not addressing these situations. Let's not be absolutists about absolutes! As with other devices, EMA is best used judiciously and thoughtfully, not as dogma. Let's focus our efforts on the situations where absolutes can do real harm...

Think how religious and political wars feed on beliefs as *everlasting, complete, final, pure,* and/or *eternal*? Would Protestants and Catholics have fought such bitter wars, leading to the deaths of millions, if not for beliefs they thought were *true* and set them against ideas they thought *intolerable*? How many ugly theories require the idea of a *pure* race? Or that *all* people of a *certain* type are such and such? How better off would people be if they put aside notions of *truth* and *ultimate* answers? And instead they accepted that their beliefs were contingent—on where they grew up and when, on their genetic gifts, etc.? How much more tolerant would people be of each other if they checked their absolutes?

The stakes can be very high indeed, but EMA can work small wonders in simple everyday living as well. You will know there is no *perfect* house, or *perfect* job or *perfect* school. You will be more circumspect before declaring that you will *never* eat at that restaurant again, or that you will *never* read Plato. You might think twice before you say how *all* Steeler fans are obnoxious, that your view on abortion is *fixed*, or that a problem is *insoluble*.

I like another example Read gives in his paper. He taught a course called "Problems in English Usage" at Columbia University for over 20 years. People have certain ideas about what is *correct* English, which implies, somehow, that there is a fixed thing out there called English. Whereas English is a creation of people communicating, an ever-changing result going back who knows how many thousands of years, and that it continues to evolve naturally over time. Instead, we might say there is a way of using English that is appropriate for our time and place (space-time).

The same carries over to spelling. As Read writes, The commoner phrase 'correct spelling' creates a false impression toward language. "If spelling is either correct or incorrect," Read wisely warns, "then that same standard can be applied to other things too."

Instead, we might say there are "conventional spellings of certain words" or "traditional spellings" which help fight off that urge to make a final judgment. Read is worth quoting fully on this point:

> If someone asks you, "What is the correct spelling of so-and-so?" you would do a social service by giving a polite but evasive reply. "Well, the usual spelling that has developed among writers of English is so-and-so." Your inquirer might be interested to learn that a common word like *good* has been spelled in thirteen different ways, according to the Oxford English Dictionary, with seven more from Scottish usage. But, you should add, it has become conventional to write g-o-o-d.

I love this careful, thoughtful way of handling ideas that is common among GS thinkers. It is a form of enlightenment, it seems to me, to be able to do this naturally—when GS becomes second nature. We can all work to get better at using these tools and the payoff comes with wisdom and tolerance and the grace that seems to flow from "self-actualized, fully-human individuals."

Here is a partial list of some words Read says we should do without:

absolutely	eternity	interminable
all	everlasting	intolerable
always	final	irresistible
beginning	fixed	never
certain	forever	perfection
certainty	immovable	perfectly
complete	impregnable	Platonic form
correct	incorrigible	pure
endless	ineradicable	total
essence	infallible	truth
eternal	insoluble	ultimate

Read is not alone in his denying of absolutes. He cites Alfred North Whitehead, who wrote in *Process and Reality*: "In philosophical discussion, the merest hint of dogmatic certainty as to finality of statement is an exhibition of folly." Read adds that Korzybski highlighted this passage in magenta in his own copy, making it stand out from his other highlights. Korzybski obviously thought it important and added in the margins "not with a date"—thereby showing how absolutes can also be tamed with his devices. For example, you might say something seems *correct* as of 2021. Korzybski's devices naturally tend to lead one to use EMA.

As I say, using the devices and being mindful of EMA has had a big impact on my own speech and thought. You may detect it in my letters to you. Not that I don't occasionally slip. Everyone does. Even Korzybski. But using these tools will enhance your time-binding skills.

Your Fellow Time-Binder,
Chris

P.S. The French essayist Michel de Montaigne (1533–1592) would've appreciated EMA. He peppered his writings liberally with EMA phrasings such as "I think" "it seems to me" "to some extent" and "perhaps." Montaigne used these terms to "soften and moderate the rashness of our propositions," as he put it.

Montaigne was a great admirer of the philosophy of Greek Skepticism, in particular its founding thinker Pyrrho and its "definitive codifier" (to use Professor Phillip Hallie's apt description), the Greek doctor and philosopher Sextus Empiricus. Their philosophy was one characterized by *epoché* or suspension of judgment. The Skeptics aimed to live peacefully, free from dogma and fanaticism about things that could not be proved. They sought what they called *ataraxia*, a state of tranquility.

Sarah Bakewell, author of a compelling Montaigne biography titled *How to Live*, tells us he had a series of medals struck with the phrase *epoché*, along with his own arms and a depiction of scales (a Pyrrhonian symbol denoting the weighing of arguments). Montaigne used these medals as reminders of the Skeptical orientation he sought to achieve in his own daily conduct.

It seems to me such an easy-going philosophy goes well with EMA. And I also suspect that consistent application of EMA also brings with it a sort of *ataraxia*. EMA helps us avoid pointless arguments. And it helps prevent our own thoughts from ossifying into dogma.

Finally, I always enjoy stumbling on insights from the past that echo, in some similar form, in GS. The roots of GS are far older than Korzybski, as he well knew.

Letter 15

E-Prime

Dear Fellow Time-Binder,

I agree with you that EMA is easy to apply.

Read's AMA reminds me of another attempt by a GS teacher to delete certain words from our vocabulary. This one is not so easy to apply. And it's controversial, even in GS circles. I am not a big fan of it as something to use regularly. But I think it has value as a training aid, as something to think about. It's called E-Prime.

D. David Bourland, Jr. (1928–2000) was the architect of this idea. He published the concept in a 1965 essay, "A Linguistic Note: Writing in E-Prime," and it set off a great deal of commentary ever since.

Bourland had been part of the GS story for years before he published his paper. He attended IGS seminars beginning in 1949. He did some volunteer work for the Institute and was even awarded a fellowship to study with Korzybski. He has the distinction of being the last person to meet with Korzybski in the latter's official capacity as director of the Institute. According to Kodish, Korzybski's biographer, Bourland met with Korzybski at 5 o'clock in the afternoon at the Institute. At 5:15, Bourland came out and called for help. "Korzybski had collapsed and was now unconscious," Kodish wrote. Korzybski died in the wee hours of the following day.

Bourland would later edit the *General Semantics Bulletin* for a time and eventually acted as a trustee for the Institute.

Anyway, in Bourland's re-telling of the story, he got the idea of E-Prime in September of 1949 while on a fellowship at the Institute. Bourland read a letter by a man—whose name is since lost—who made the suggestion of doing without "to be." That's all E-Prime is: English without any form of the verb "to be." That means doing without *be, is, am, are, was, were, been* and *being*.

Now, this may seem a strange suggestion, but it has a history. Korzybski himself wrote about the idea in *S&S*: "The little word 'to be' appears a very peculiar word and is, perhaps, responsible for many human semantic difficulties."

And he was not alone. Bourland lists an impressive array of other thinkers who have "struggled with the semantic consequences of the verb to be for hundreds of years." These include Thomas Hobbes, Augustus de Morgan,

Bertrand Russell, Alfred North Whitehead, and George Santayana.

Why?

Let us consider the word "is." If I say, "Rapoport is smart," it seems as if "smartness" is some kind of attribute affixed to Rapoport. What I really mean is "Rapoport seems smart to me." And as an aside, we can use Rapoport's operational philosophy to get at what I mean by smart. Or, to put the question operationally, "what sort of actions or thoughts do I associate with 'smart'?" But I digress—more on Rapoport and operational philosophy in a future letter...

Any sort of use of the word "is" risks conflating a point-of-view with some kind of objective attribute inherent in the event described. This is the sort of thing Korzybski wanted us to avoid doing. E-Prime is an attempt to accomplish Korzybski's wish. Bourland considered E-Prime an "offshoot of Korzybski's system." (In GS literature, you find people talking about the 'is of identity' the 'is of predication.' But I fail to see the value added in making this distinction and so ignore it. Better to just have a gentle alarm bell ring when you see the word 'is.')

E-Prime would have us restate our opinion of Rapoport in this following way: "Rapoport *seems* smart," or even "Rapoport *seems* smart *to me*."

The psychologist Rollo May made an interesting observation in his *The Discovery of Being* (1983). He wrote that "Eastern languages, such as Japanese, adjectives always include the implication of for-me-ness. That is to say, 'this flower is beautiful' means 'for me this flower is beautiful.'"

E-Prime would have our language mirror that sense of "for-me-ness" or "to-me-ness." In these letters, we've talked about how GS, in part, aims to improve our "maps" (our descriptions, theories, etc.), then you can readily see how E-Prime helps. A rose is not red, technically speaking. A particular rose may seem red to you.

As Robert Anton Wilson put it, "any sentence containing the innocent-looking 'is' also contains a hidden fallacy." I am reminded of a funny story Edmund Carpenter tells—in *Oh, What A Blow That Phantom Game Me!*—about a time he was traveling with an Inuit hunter name Ohnainewk in the frigid Northwest Territories. Carpenter says "the wind is cold." And Ohnainewk laughs and says "How can the *wind* be cold? You're cold... but the wind isn't cold..."

In other ways, E-Prime can help avoid us making unnecessarily dogmatic assertions. For example, E-Prime will not allow you to say: "There is no solution to this problem." Instead, it forces you to recast the assertion in "for-me-ness" terms. You could say, "I don't see a solution to this problem (as of now)." The latter is a more accurate map, you might say, of the situation at hand.

E-Prime can prevent erroneous presumptions from taking on the appearance of a 'fact.' You can't say, "Harry is drunk." But you can say, "Harry seems drunk to me." The E-Prime version leaves an obvious window of doubt and almost invites room for testing and revision.

Bourland sums up (in a later paper "To be or not to be: A tool for critical thinking") the ways in which E-Prime helps us make better maps:

- Everything in the 'real world' changes: Sometimes so rapidly that we may not notice the changes directly (as in the case of a table which appears solid), sometimes so slowly that we can (as in the case of a river).
- Every person, as well as every 'thing,' undergoes such changes.
- One particular verb in English—to be—carries with it archaic associations and implications of permanence and static existence that we do not find in the 'real world.'

I agree with all of these and I would say they succinctly sum up why it's useful to know something about E-Prime. I can say from my own experience that time spent working with E-Prime has been fruitful—not because I go around not using forms of "to be," but simply because familiarity with E-Prime does often make me pause over those "to be" forms. I will often substitute a "seems to me" over an "is" when I think it is important to convey "to-me-ness." Even if I use "is" I will often qualify it. I might say "Amazon's stock is a good investment, it *seems to me*."

But passions can run high when it comes to E-Prime and there is quite extensive literature on it. There are advocates of speaking in E-Prime. There is E-Prime fiction. There are attempts to re-write historical documents using E-Prime, etc. Some notable authors have written entire books in E-Prime, including Robert Anton Wilson and Albert Ellis.

However, I find myself in agreement with Stuart Mayper, another wise GS teacher. First, he had some good things to say about E-Prime: "[It] does force us to think about [language's] structure rather than rattle on in habitual patterns; it reveals some hidden assumptions; it toughens (though sometimes lengthens) our sentences."

But otherwise, he argued against using E-Prime as some kind of default setting on language use. There is a funny story Susan Presby Kodish tells about Mayper in this regard. She is the co-author, along with her husband Bruce Kodish, of a useful book on GS called *Drive Yourself Sane*:

When asked to read and comment on the first draft of our book, *Drive Yourself Sane*, Stuart's first comment was something like, "I was relieved when I got to the second chapter." Uh oh, what was wrong with the first chapter? Nothing. Rather, his relief came with the first "is" in the second chapter; having seen none in the first chapter, he was worried that we were writing it in E-Prime. What a delightful (and typically sly) way to express his Opinion.

I think the best arguments against using E-Prime as a default setting were cobbled together by another GS writer, James French in his piece "The Top Ten Arguments Against E-Prime." I won't go through all of them here but his number #1 argument and it seems a clincher for me:

> E-Prime makes no distinction between statements that cross the principles of general semantics and statements that do not. A statement such as, "I am going to the store," violates no formulation of general semantics, yet E-Prime prohibits it. That clearly places E-Prime outside the interrelated set of principles and practices that constitute the discipline.

Nonetheless, since you know about EMA, you might as well know about E-Prime. It can be a useful tool, much like Korzyski's devices, just don't go overboard.

Your Fellow Time-Binder,

Chris

Letter 16
Either/Or

Dear Fellow Time-Binder,

As I read over my last letter to you, I am naturally led to think of another GS tool to share: Either/Or—it's almost an extension of EMA. GS suggests caution when dealing with either/or thinking. Instead, we want to embrace a multi-valued orientation. I'll show you what I mean in this letter.

And yes, you are right to wonder when I am going to write more about S.I. Hayakawa (1906–1992). While Korzybski founded GS as a discipline or approach, S.I. Hayakawa brought it national attention. So I am not entirely surprised you've heard of him.

Hayakawa would go on to become a US Senator, after all, and achieve some measure of fame when he yanked the plug on the loudspeakers of student protestors at a highly charged outdoor rally at San Francisco State College in the late 1960s. (Hayakawa was an English professor there.) And he is the author of a book— *Language in Thought and Action*—that became a Book-of-the-month selection, a bestseller with over one million copies sold and one that is still in print today in its 5th edition. For a lot of people, Hayakawa was their introduction to Korzybskian ideas.

Hayakawa was a student of Korzybski's, attending seminars in 1938, and acknowledged his "deepest debt" to Korzybski in his famous book. Hayakawa was also the editor of *ETC*, the main organ of GS ideas, from 1943 to 1970. He could be witty in his editorship. He once accidentally attributed an article on law and semantics to the wrong legal-semanticist. In his apology in the next issue, Hayakawa wrote he had unconsciously identified "legal-semanticist$_1$ with legal-semanticist$_2$..."

As editor of *ETC*, he also oversaw a lively letters section. So, he's a substantial figure in the GS firmament.

Unfortunately, Korzybski and Hayakawa had a strained relationship that sort of split GS into two camps for a while. I don't see much point in going over this ground, but I do want to acknowledge it because the GS of Hayakawa is not quite the GS of Korzybski. These differences, like doctrinal differences among Christians, can be most heated. (You can find more about their differences in the biographies of both men. Korzybski's biography, which I've already referred to, is by Bruce Kodish. Hayakawa's biography is by one of his students, *In Thought and Action: The Enigmatic Life of S. I. Hayakawa* by Gerald W. Haslam with Janice E. Haslam.)

My favorite version of Hayakawa's famous book is the original one, published in 1941. In a later preface, Hayakawa writes about the purpose of this first edition. It's worth quoting in full here:

> The original version of this book, Language in Action, published in 1941, was in many respects a response to the dangers of propaganda, especially as exemplified in Adolf Hitler's success in persuading millions to share his maniacal and destructive views. It was the writer's conviction then, as it remains now, that everyone needs to have a habitually critical attitude towards language—his own as well as that of others—both for the sake of his personal well being and for his adequate functioning as a citizen. Hitler is gone, but if the majority of our fellow citizens are more susceptible to the slogans of fear and race hatred than to those of peaceful accommodation and mutual respect among human beings, our political liberties remain at the mercy of any eloquent and unscrupulous demagogue.

The shadow of war hangs over the early GS literature, naturally because it developed in the aftermath of WWI and rose to prominence against a backdrop that included the rise of Nazism, fascism, and WWII. All of which reminds us that the consequences of errant time-binding—cross-binding—can be severe. (Hayakawa said his own interest in GS "developed as a result of my excitement about the rise of Hitler in the 1930s.")

I like to remind people of this because the biggest pushback I get from friends (and friendly critics) is that GS tells us things that are obvious and, hence, its concerns are somehow trivial. I could not disagree more.

Shortly after the first atomic bombs were used to kill hundreds of thousands of Japanese people, Korzybski wrote "Release of Atomic Energy," in which he made the following point:

> That knowledge [which led to the release of atomic energy] was due to the uniquely human capacities of transmitting "knowledge" from generation to generation, not present in any other form of life. I called that human capacity Time-binding, in my *Manhood of Humanity* (1921). All science goes that way, and empirical results speak for themselves, destructively or constructively.

The consequences for our own time and those of our children and grandchildren, may well be just as high. Our challenges are no less immense—racism, religious fanaticism, bitter political divisions, the ill effects of huge disparities in wealth, climate change, etc. GS can help us think through all of these areas.

Hayakawa, as it happens, wrote well on this topic of Either/Or, which I want to focus on in this letter. Now, "either/or" thinking, or a two-valued orientation, is quite common. And to be fair, in a lot of cases, it is harmless or even necessary. As for the former, if somebody asks me if I'd like to play golf on Saturday afternoon, I expect I'll say "yes" or "no." Or somebody might ask me if I like pizza, I'll probably say yes. (It's my favorite food.) These are inconsequential social communications, and we're not addressing those.

However, there are lots of cases where the consequences can be dire. For example, political and religious bigotry depends on either/or thinking. You are either a "for us" or "against us." You are either a "Republican" or a "Democrat." Think of the many ways we divide humanity with either/or type thinking.

Hayakawa writes about how Hitler used either/or thinking to separate people and advance his agenda—"Jews" versus "Aryans." Or think about how Japanese people were immediately cast under suspicion during WWII and interned. The underlying principle of two-valued thinking is that there is no middle ground.

GS encourages multi-valued thinking. As you might guess, a multi-valued orientation sees more than two values. Every quarrel has not two sides, but many. True to basic GS principles, a multi-valued orientation seems to better reflect most life situations. Hayakawa talks about how people want all kinds of things. They want to make money, have friends, eat well, sleep soundly, etc. Some things they want more than other things. A multi-valued orientation sees people as the complex bundle of ideas, opinions, wants, and needs that they seem to be.

In any controversy, two-valued thinking has a way of polluting discussion. Debates devolve into exaggerated claims and rhetoric. It becomes a show about who "won." Ideas are shorn of any intellectual weight.

"There are people that object to this shilly-shallying," Hayakawa writes, "and insist on 'an outright yes or no.' They are the Gordian knot cutters; they may undo the knot, but they ruin the rope."

A multi-valued orientation is already embedded in the language of science and mathematics. As Hayakawa points out, we don't have to rely on words such as "hot" or "cold"; we can give degrees on a fixed scale. We can use a range of measures in our descriptions—horsepower, voltage, miles per hour, etc. "The language of science," Hayakawa writes, "can be said to offer an *infinite-valued orientation*. Having at its command the means to adjust one's action in an infinite number of ways according to the exact situation at hand, science travels rapidly and gets things done."

So, my key bit of advice here is simple: Anytime you come across either/or thinking—any attempt to reduce things to just two options—let that ring a little bell in your head and pause. Ask yourself if either/or is appropriate here, or whether a multi-valued orientation would be more suitable. You'll find it opens up interesting lines of thought.

Your Fellow Time-Binder,

Chris

P.S. Ironic, perhaps, that Korzybski himself formulated his system of GS as "non-Aristotelian," thereby cleaving knowledge in two camps, the other being "Aristotelian." A contradictory and ironic manifestation of either/or thinking! Ideas are not usually so neat. So, our critique holds even against Korzybski's formulation. Systems can seem partially in both camps, by varying degrees. How useful these distinctions are I leave up to you to decide.

From my own point of view, I see the concept of Aristotelian and non-Aristotelian may have some pedagogical value, as long as one remains aware of the limitations of two-valued orientations. In any case, I don't think it is an important matter to decide one way or the other.

Letter 17
The Meaning of Words

Dear Fellow Time-Binder,

GS is not a study of the meaning of words. Better to say, as Wendell Johnson has said, that GS is more concerned with the assumptions underlying the use of words (or any symbols) and the effects of using words (or symbols generally). These are old concerns and GS builds on the work of many others who have mined the same shaft.

John Locke (1632–1704), for example, titled Chapter 10 of his great work *An Essay Concerning Human Understanding* "Of the abuse of words." He writes about the ways in which people misuse words. Among these misuses he includes words affixed to "very important ideas, without any distinct meaning at all." His examples include *wisdom*, *glory*, and *grace*.

Another misuse Locke identifies sounds a Korzybskian note: taking words for things. Locke particularly criticizes philosophers for making up terms—he cites Aristotelian categories such as *substantial form* and *vegetative soul*—and treating them as if they were 'real.' "Gibberish" he calls them.

Sounding much like Korzybski would centuries later, he writes:

> We should have a great many fewer disputes in the world, if words were taken for what they are, the signs of our *ideas* only, and not for the things themselves.

Other early modern philosophers flagged these issues as well. Francis Bacon writes in *The Great Instauration* about how "words are the tokens and signs of notions. . . improperly and overhastily abstracted from facts." And Thomas Hobbes (1588–1679) writes of "senseless and ambiguous words. . . [are] like *ignes fatus* [fool's fire], and reasoning upon them is a wandering amongst innumerable absurdities."

So you see, GS concerns enjoy a rich heritage in the history of ideas, one that even many GS adherents overlook. Not all, however. Irving Lee, for one, encouraged familiarity with this relevant historical literature. He devised a survey of ten books and included among them the works of Bacon, Hobbes, and Locke. Never let it be said that GS is philosophically underfed.

Back to words: Since GS doesn't study meanings per se, it follows that GS is not so interested in definitions, as such. But we are interested in the assumptions we make about what words mean and how we formulate such definitions. Let me show you what I mean.

In GS, we talk about terms being *over/under* defined. Most terms are over/under defined. To understand this, think back to the concepts of *intensional* and *extensional*. If I ask you "What is a house?" and you give me a dictionary definition, that would be an intensional definition. If instead you pointed at a "house" nearby, that would be an extensional definition. If we rely on a dictionary definition for a "house," we will find that the definition is not adequate, say, when we go buy a house. The definition is too limited and leaves out too many details. If we rely on the extensional definition, we are at the other extreme—lots of details in the particular house you pointed out will not carry over when we look at other houses. Korzybski gives many examples of over/under-defined terms: dollar, gold, god, war, peace, education, teacher, genius, among others.

Perhaps another way to better understand the idea is (ironically) from a definition by S.I. Hayakawa and Anatol Rapoport:

> Most definitions, other than mathematical, over (under) define terms in the sense that less (more) is included in the definition than was intended. That is, however one defines, for example, 'classical music,' the definition will necessarily both include things that one did not want to include, and excluded things one did not want to exclude.

Boiled down to its basics, you might say all the above is a glorified attempt to simply say "the meanings of most words are ambiguous." Maybe so. But I believe the added color in this letter shows you *why* they are ambiguous.

It is important to note that Korzybski is not saying to avoid using ambiguous words. As Irving Lee writes, we might be tempted to divide words into two categories, A and B:

A. The use of ambiguous, abstract, vague, generalized, imprecise, inaccurate, fanciful, imaginative statements.
B. The use of concrete, specific, precise, definite, accurate, realistic statements.

But, as Lee says, "Korzybski never (to my knowledge) urged that men speak in terms of B to the exclusion of A. What he did say was this: Men must know what and whereof they speak. They must know the difference between the A and B forms."

Another way words are ambiguous is in their *multi-ordinal* character. To understand this powerful idea, I want to bring in another of the stars in Korzybski's orbit: J. Samuel Bois (pronounced "Bwa"). I mentioned him in an earlier letter as the guy who delivered the first IGS lectures after Korzybski died, which shows you how well he was regarded at the time as a practitioner and teacher of GS.

Bois (1892–1978), was born in a cabin in the settlement of Stratford Centre, in Quebec, Canada. He went on to become a Catholic priest and Jesuit. He wasn't the quiet type however, as he organized labor unions, started a weekly Catholic newspaper, and did missionary work among the Mexicans and Native Americans of California. But Bois also proved to be someone who would not just accept another's wholesale beliefs uncritically. He began to teach ideas not quite in line with the dogma of the Church. After 14 years as a priest, the Church condemned him and discharged him from the clergy.

So, in 1936 at the age of 44, he began the next phase of his life. He got a PhD in psychology and, along with a colleague, they opened the first psychological consulting practice in Canada. In 1939 he discovered GS and read Korzybski's *S&S*, which he studied with "feverish eagerness." He joined the Canadian army in 1941 and took the book with him, studying it almost daily.

After the war, he attended his first Korzybski seminar in 1945. By 1947 he himself was giving lectures at the Institute. He wrote the GS classic *The Art of Awareness*, initially published in 1966 and subsequently revised (and still in print in its 4th edition). This book is generally regarded as one of the classic works of GS and still holds up today.

And here I want to get back to the idea of multi-ordinal, which Bois makes particularly clear and also sees as very important ("epoch-making," as he says). So what does it mean? A word is multi-ordinal when that word, without changing its dictionary definition, can refer to different orders of abstraction.

Bois gives an example. When we say individual, family, state, and nation, we are unlikely to get confused about orders of abstraction. But what if we use the word "unit." Unit could refer to any of these abstractions—i.e, an individual unit, a family unit, etc.

Bois writes about how in the army "unit" could refer to a platoon, a company, a battalion, etc. Multi-ordinal terms resist general definitions. Compare the word 'fact' with the word 'chair.' The latter is fairly definite most of the time. We can point to a piece of furniture and call it 'chair.' But 'fact' is multi-ordinal most of the time—it is impossible to pin down a definition that is 'good' in all cases.

I like Bois' example from the stock market. We might say the Dow Jones

Industrial Average was down today. So, "stocks are down" is a 'fact.' But it is also a 'fact'—of a different order—that the Dow was up over the last year ("stocks are up"). Bois called the first notion ("stocks are down") a content; and the latter ("stock are up") the container (perhaps because the former is a fact nested in a larger container). In this way, multi-ordinal terms can be both content and container.

Another example is the word 'manager.' People in an organization can both be a manager and have a manager themselves. Once you get the idea of multi-ordinal, you start to see there are many such terms. Multi-ordinal terms do a lot of work for us, so we don't have to invent new terms to describe every ambiguous case. But we should be conscious of these words.

"The old prescription 'define your terms' does not apply to multi-ordinal terms," as Bois wrote, "and, because there are so many multi-ordinal terms and so frequently used, this prescription is now recognized as a most burdensome and useless legacy of Aristotelian logic."

Instead of asking "what is a fact?" or "what is management?" Bois directs us to think about the order of abstraction we're dealing with. He asks us to think about *who*, *what*, *when*, *where*, and *how*.

Bois created a diagram that illustrates multi-ordinality, as units of a lower order within units of a higher order. The horizontal line represents our first-order experience, or as Bois calls it "the down-to-earth level of contact with what is going on." Multi-ordinal words nest like Russian dolls, and clear thinking demands we keep the levels of abstraction distinct when using multi-ordinal terms. (See diagram on next page.)

The diagram, Bois wrote, "lends itself to a limitless variety of applications. It gives us a visual picture of theories within theories, of decisions within decisions, and systems within systems."

In summary, the concepts of *over/under-defined* and *multi-ordinal* give us interesting ways to think about the ambiguity inherent in the meaning of words.

One last thing before I sign off: In an appreciation of Bois, Ethel Longstreet (a long-time collaborator and friend of Bois) quotes from a 1971 paper of Bois' titled "What Our Work in General Semantics Is About." I would like to share a few sentences which summarize what Bois thought GS was good for:

> It is not a matter of changing the world around us, but a matter of making the most of that limited part of the world that is within our field of influence: Our Own Self.

It is not a matter of imposing on the rest of humankind our technology and our way of life, but a matter of making available to all inhabitants of this planet the most advanced mental and physical tools that may bring about abundance, peace and self-actualization.

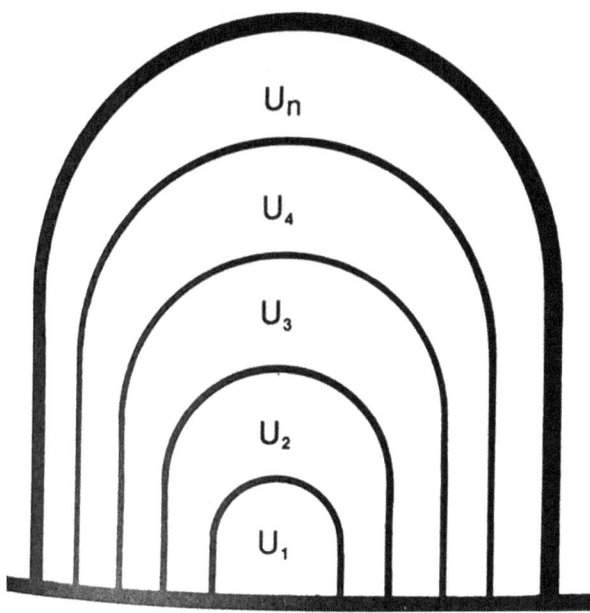

It is not a matter of repudiating as altogether false former myths, religions, and theories, but a matter of extracting from these earlier systems what kernels of everlasting wisdom they kept wrapped up in formulations that are not obsolete.

Bois gives us something to shoot for.

Your Fellow Time-Binder,

Chris

P.S. I love the extensional and intensional concepts, despite the awkwardness of the words. I believe they capture something important. Once you get used to working with them, you'll see new ways of describing, or thinking about, events. For example, James French wrote about an extensional definition of time-binding itself in the *General Semantic Bulletin 2004 Yearbook*.

So, we have a definition of time-binding by intension (a dictionary style definition). Recall what we said in an earlier letter. We called time-binding the capacity of humans to summarize, digest and appropriate the labors and experiences of the past. That's an intensional definition.

French suggested we could also define time-binding by extension. We could do this "by listing the actual results of the efforts of human generations over time, as in the random and partial list below":

1. space-flight
2. sports
3. language
4. sociology
5. agriculture
6. television
7. history
8. ethics
9. radio
10. physics
11. accounting
12. music
13. automobiles
14. cooking
15. telemetry
16. writing
17. pottery
18. theories
19. law
20. books
21. art
22. film
23. commerce
24. philosophy
25. comedy
26. metallurgy
27. ecology
28. measurement
29. money
30. clothing
31. electric lights
32. planetology
33. anthropology
34. experiments
35. democracy
36. mass production
37. cloth
38. telephones
39. astronomy
40. chemistry
41. robotics
42. tools
43. paper
44. cartography
45. medicine
46. automation
47. biology
48. psychiatry
49. politics
50. birth control
51. computers
52. holography
53. schools
54. mathematics
55. statistics
56. weapons
57. calendars
58. poetry
59. lasers
60. religion

What a neat way to give a rich extensional meaning to time-binding.

Letter 18

Operational Philosophy

Dear Fellow Time-Binder,

If I had to offer a general principle regarding the definition of words, I'd say: The meaning of words are in the way people use them. The words themselves have no meaning, or power, save what people grant them.

And yet, the importance of keeping one's definitions straight also seems important, less we risk, as Thomas Hobbes wrote, getting "entangled in words; as a bird in lime twigs, the more he struggles, the more belimed."

We've already seen the weakness of a dictionary definition, defining words with more words. We've talked about extensional definitions, by contrast, which are richer but not easy to articulate. Using some combination of the two seems a path to an enlightened use of words.

There is another way to think about these questions. For this, I'd like to introduce you to another thinker in the GS circle: Anatol Rapoport (1911–2007).

Rapoport was born in Ukraine and came to the United States in 1922. He became a capable mathematician and would contribute to a variety of fields including game theory. Rapoport would write over 300 papers about over two dozen books in his lifetime. He was a gifted pianist and peace activist as well.

My favorite Rapoport anecdote has to do with his "tit-for-tat" strategy. In 1980, Robert Axelrod, organized a computer tournament to explore cooperation strategies in the framework of the prisoner's dilemma. (Axelrod would go on to publish an important book on this subject, called *The Evolution of Cooperation*.)

The prisoner's dilemma is a famous puzzle involving two prisoners in solitary confinement, unable to communicate with each other. The cops are trying to get a confession out of them both. Here are the various ways the situation will play out:

- If A and B each betray the other, each of them serves two years in prison.
- If A betrays B but B remains silent, A will be set free, and B will serve three years in prison.

- If A remains silent but B betrays A, A will serve three years in prison, and B will be set free
- If A and B both remain silent, both of them will serve only one year in prison (on the lesser charge).

That's the standard set-up, and so the question is, what do you do?

Axelrod invited well-known game theorists to submit strategies that a computer could run. For example, you might pursue a random strategy, or you might always cooperate, etc. In the tournament, the strategies would all be run against each other and themselves, repeatedly.

Well, the winner of the tournament was Rapoport's simple strategy, called tit-for-tat. This strategy would cooperate on the first move and then for every mover thereafter it would copy whatever its opponent did last. Hence, tit-for-tat.

Then, Axelrod announced the winner and let all the game theorists submit another program. Rapoport submitted his tit-for-tat strategy again... and won again. Rapoport's was the simplest submitted—and won both times.

From the *Globe & Mail* in 2007 (the year of Rapoport's death):

> "In effect, Tit-For-Tat punished the other player for selfish behavior and rewarded her for co-operative behavior — but the punishment lasted only as long as the selfish behavior lasted," observed Metta Spencer, editor of Peace Magazine, on the occasion of Dr. Rapoport's 90th birthday. "This proved to be an exceptionally effective sanction, quickly showing the other side the advantages of co-operating... It also set moral philosophers to proposing this as a workable principle to use in real life interactions."

He was, suffice it to say, an accomplished and brilliant character. But let's back up a bit and see how he came to GS.

As a young man, Rapoport studied music and pursued a career as a concert pianist. He toured the United States, Europe, and Mexico in the 1930s, but then gave up on the idea of becoming a pianist as a career. He enrolled in the University of Chicago and eventually earned a Ph.D. in mathematics 1941, the same year he joined the US Army.

He served in the Air Corps, first in Alaska. Sometime while in the service, he read Korzybski's *Science & Sanity*. Rapoport was certainly taken with Korzybski's GS and an interest in GS would be part of his life from that point afterwards (and the subject of a few of his books). While in the Air Corps, he wrote a paper applying some of Korzybksi's ideas called "Newtonian Physics and Aviation Cadets," which he submitted to *ETC*, then edited by Hayawaka. Hayakawa thought it a fine article and published it. Korzybski also liked the article.

Rapoport showed he had a sense of humor in a letter he wrote in early 1945 to ETC, while still serving in the Air Corps (Capt.). He was in India in a camp where the food was "particularly vile." Then Rapoport trotted out some of his recent GS learning. He pointed out to his fellows, who complained about the food, "$hash_{Monday}$ was NOT identical with $hash_{Tuesday}$. Neither was $hash_{dinner}$ identical with $hash_{supper}$." He continued: "The recognition of this elementary truth was all that was needed to change a seemingly unbearable monotonous diet into a richly varied one." The editor, presumably the witty Hayakawa, slapped a clever title on the letter: "Still Hash!"

Rapoport finally met Hayakawa in person in 1945 in Chicago after the war. Hayakawa invited him to co-edit *ETC*, and the two became close friends. Hayakawa wrote the foreword to Rapoport's first book, *Science and the Goals of Man* (1950). I mentioned the strained relationship between Hayakawa and Korzybski; well Rapoport entered into that conflict on the Hayakawa side. Rapoport could be overly critical of Korzybski to the point where it seems personal.

In any event, I have enjoyed Rapoport's writings, and his best book may be *Operational Philosophy* (published in 1953 and re-published in 1969 by the International Society for General Semantics).

Rapoport's operational philosophy ("OP" henceforth) sees language as a way of organizing experience. What makes words usable is they have definitions. OP aims to, as he puts it, "make some connection between a word and experience, not merely between a word and other words."

Does this remind you of Korzybski and extensional definitions? "What is a house?" An extensional definition would be not merely words, but also a pointing at something—that building over there, or even a picture. But sometimes we can only rely on defining words in terms of other words. "Success" is not a word we can define by pointing. (Well, maybe you can. . .)

And so, a good operational definition is one that gets as close to experience as possible using words. Moreover—and this is important—the definition is in tune with the person you are trying to communicate with.

Rapoport gives the example of time. What is time? To a child, you might explain it by talking about the change in seasons, the marking off of days on a calendar or the effects of aging. To an adult, you might just say, "Time is what we measure with a clock"—a practical, and operational, definition. This definition ties back to a shared experience we have with other people. To a physicist, a good operational definition of time might be "the independent variable in the differential equation of motion."

For some words, it could take some work to attain an operational definition. If someone says they want to be successful, then you have to ask a follow-up question to try to pin down what "successful" means to this person. Eventually, you might determine that success to this person means having a six-figure salary—a shallow definition of success, but a working operational definition that allows you to understand what this person means when they use that word.

Rapoport's OP has a way of shifting your focus. Certain questions that pose problems can be restated such that you can give an operational answer. For example, consider the question "What is real?" Rapoport offers a restatement using OP: "To what sort of experience do people usually refer when they say something is 'real'?"

Now we have a question one can work to answer in a useful way. There may be some criteria we can accept for saying something is 'real.' This is no different than how we use lots of other words. Consider the word "pencil." You have a bank of experiences using pencils, seeing pencils, etc. And I have a different bank of experiences with "pencils." But there are some broad criteria about pencils that we both accept. Hence, we can use that word and understand what each other means—even though we may never have had the exact same experience of the exact same pencil.

Rapoport uses the term "relativity of meaning" to refer to the variability of experience in a word (i.e., different kinds of pencils). And he uses "invariance" to indicate common bases of experience. So, "east" and "west" are defined conventions that have a certain invariance. If we were standing facing each other, "east" might be on my left and your right. That's the relativity of meaning. But we would both agree, directionally, which way was "east." That's the invariant part of "east."

Or consider temperature. On a particularly sunny day, a Bostonian may feel it is warm and go outside in shorts and t-shirt. But a Floridian might think it chilly and wear a light sweater. How the temperature feels that day is relative. However, both the Bostonian and Floridian can look at a thermometer and agree that it says 60 degrees Fahrenheit. That's the invariant part.

The quest for meaning or definitions, then, is really a quest for invariants.

So, the property of weight has invariance. . . because we have scales. "If the only way we can be aware of the amount of weight is by means of a scale," Raporport writes, "then the very definition of weight has to be in terms of the scale."

The idea of a "true weight" is kind of fanciful then. Because what someone weighs depends on the scale. It also depends on when and where you weigh them. The point being that we can talk about weight in a meaningful way because we're willing to forgo a certain precision. In Rapoport's terms, we'd say, "what do people mean when they talk about how much they weigh?" And we have an acceptable criteria in saying a person weighs whatever a scale says when they step on it.

I like OP because of the way it roots your questions in practical, real-world considerations. I like how it checks inclinations to get too attached to the abstractions embedded in questions. Too often, people throw around questions such as "What is fair?" and take for granted that "fairness" has a useful meaning. OP makes us work at getting an operational definition.

As Rapoport says, "The important thing about operational definitions is that they tell *what to do* and *what to observe* in order to bring the thing defined or its (invariant) effects within the range of one's experience." OP doesn't let you assume the invariants are there. You have to figure them out.

Sincerely,

Chris

P.S. You remember the *X-Files* tagline? "The truth is out there." Well, the 'truth' is never out there, as philosopher Richard Rorty reminds us in *Contingency, Irony and Solidarity*. "The world is out there," he wrote, "but descriptions of the world are not." We make descriptions of that world, which are not found in the world itself. And only descriptions can be (in the operational sense) 'true,' 'false,' 'indeterminate' or 'meaningless.'

These descriptions, crafted by human nervous systems, can be judged and compared against other descriptions by human nervous systems. "The world does not speak," Rorty wrote, "only we do." We replace certain descriptions (the earth is flat) with better descriptions (the earth is round). And better means more useful. A better description allows us to do more things, to talk about more things, explain more events, make better predictions, etc.

Ergo, there is no objective world out there, no final arbiter of descriptions where we say "ah, that's it, we have it pinned down now." We can never have it pinned down. We can always replace one description with another description. (I use the absolutes advisedly here.) Moreover, it is not always easy to know which description is "better." Even in physics, there are great debates about all kinds of theories. And what passes for "best description" today can be bettered tomorrow as Einstein 'improved' on Newton, and as quantum mechanics 'bettered' Einsteinian physics in some respects. It doesn't mean the old way was 'wrong' or 'untrue'—it simply means a more useful description, in the way we've been talking about it, has emerged.

In the social realm of politics, practical living, religions, etc., there are a profusion of descriptions. Which description of the world is "better"— the one offered by the Democratic Party or Republican Party? Which description is better, the one offered by the Stoics or the Epicureans? Which description is better, the one offered by Christians or Hindus?

The key point here is that there is no "final vocabulary," as Rorty put it. I think even GS writers can sometimes give the impression that the territory is an objective thing against which we can check our maps. The map is not the territory... but the territory is not something we can know in all its ever-changing details, as Korzybski's SD makes clear. We're always making inferences based on what we can detect. Knowing this should both keep us humble with regard to our currently held descriptions (both those borrowed or learned from others and those we make for ourselves from our own experiences) and more open-minded about the descriptions of others.

Thanks to Rorty, I now imagine, even when reading the works of philosophers and other thinkers, that I am reading the works of poets. A philosopher, such as Spinoza or Schopenhauer, is a poet of a kind. (See, for example, his *Philosophy as Poetry*). Philosophers offer a way to see the world. But for us, there should be no pressure to decide who was 'right.' We can enjoy what they offer in the same spirit we would enjoy Keats or Bukowski.

In this view, new theories and ideas are not representations of the 'real world,' not maps of an objective territory, but they are "poetic achievements," to use Rorty's phrase. The question of which set of maps is 'right' need not arise. "The answer to a great poem is a still better poem," Rorty wrote.

Our imaginations, our ability to interpret and create, propel us to write more poems, to make progress—the sort of progress embedded in the concept of time-binding, where the result is a richer treasury of descriptions from which to choose and more recipes to build and tinker with—all unburdened by the notion that there is a "final answer" at which such progress must stop.

Letter 19

Non-Additivity and True, False, Indeterminate, and Meaningless

Dear Fellow Time-Binder,

If you want to explore more about operational philosophy, I would definitely recommend you read Rapoport's book (*Operational Philosophy*, of course).

He wrote other books too. I remember I was initially put off by him because he seemed to be unfairly critical of Korzybski. He called Korzybski a "crackpot" more than once and seemed to have a real problem with Korzybski's writing style. And yet, he could be effusive with praise to the point of embarrassing hyperbole—like when he said Korzybski "was the precursor of an intellectual revolution unequaled since the renaissance."

But I got over this hurdle, and I am glad I did. Rapoport's book adds worthwhile techniques to the GS toolbox. I'll give you another example from *Operational Philosophy*. You may recall, some letters back, we talked about how we want to be careful with "either/or" thinking.

Along the same lines, we want to handle words like 'true' and 'false' with care. What is 'true' really? Now this can take us into deep philosophical waters, but let us skirt the shallows for a moment because what I'm about to tell you is worth sharing.

Rapoport is a good non-Aristotelian and pushes back against categorical terms such as 'truth.' "What is truth?" framed operationally would instead be "What sorts of acceptable criteria can we agree on for something to qualify as true?" This is far trickier than it seems. Even statements that seem unquestionably 'true' dissolve under scrutiny.

I remember discussing this with a friend, who said there are statements one can make that are unquestionably 'true.' I asked him to name one. He came up with the Pythagorean theorem, which states that the hypotenuse of a triangle is equal to the sum of the areas of the squares on the other two sides.

'True'? Not always. The Pythagorean theorem is fundamental to Euclidean geometry, but that doesn't make it 'true' in the world as we experience it. Euclidean geometry depends on idealized forms. As Buckminster Fuller liked to point out, there are no straight lines, squares, triangles, etc. in nature. Euclidean geometry works as an approximation, but it is not always 'true.' There are, in fact, other non-Euclidean geometries, as we've mentioned in previous letters.

But you may understand my objection with a simpler example. Consider the statement 1 + 1 = 2. Is that always true? Well, in the world as we experience it, we can take one gallon of water and add one gallon of alcohol. . . and the resulting liquid will be something less than two gallons (of greater density). Korzybski used this example in his book *S&S*. (And he points to other examples where non-additivity applies, such as in dealing with temperature or density.) Weinberg, another GS teacher we've mentioned before, goes so far as to say that "on the non-verbal level, 1 + 1 never equals 2 exactly."

Perhaps Weinberg's statement is too strong—"never" seems inadvisable for a general semanticist to use, although I use it at times!—but when I think about it, I am hard pressed to find an exception. Taking one carrot and adding another carrot doesn't make two carrots *exactly*—not on the "nonverbal level," which is the key qualifier. The second carrot is different from the first.

In this, we get to another GS principle—the principle of *non-additivity*. It means exactly what Weinberg says it means. The non-additivity principle may not seem important when you add one carrot to another and say you have two carrots. But it can be disastrous if you ignore it in other ways. Adding "one more person" to a team is not so simple. "One more person" vastly complicates the relationships and possible connections between team members. I remember when I had a second kid, experienced parents would joke with me and say that it's not twice the work, but more like ten times the work!

Basically, the principle of non-additivity warns us of another way in which our verbal maps don't fit the territory. Our way of talking makes it seem as if relationships are simpler and less complicated than they seem to be in the process world we inhabit. Weinberg sums it up thus: "The general semanticist holds that by making ourselves explicitly aware of the non-additive character of the universe, we will be more likely to use a language whose structure implies it, and therefore we will be less likely to deceive ourselves because of the language we use to describe it."

Back to Rapoport, who has fun examples of non-additivity in his book *Science and the Goals of Man*. If it is 7 o'clock and we want to know what time it will be 14 hours from now, we understand the answer is nine o'clock. This is an instance where the statement "7 + 14 = 9" would be 'true.'

Another example comes from golf. If I walk 300 feet and then walk another 400 feet, how far would I be from my starting point? Of course, you have to know which direction I walked. And so again we have an example where 300 feet + 400 feet doesn't necessarily equal 700 feet. It might, if I walked in a straight line—which again is an idealized form. I can attest, there are no straight lines on golf courses. Not when I play!

These discussions take place in a chapter in Rapoport's book called "How Evident is Self-Evident?" To which Rapoport answers "not very."

Rapoport's operational philosophy gives us another way to think about 'true' and 'false.' Remember, OP reframes the question "What is truth?" by asking something like "what sorts of acceptable criteria can we agree on for something to qualify as true?" We're looking for those *invariants* as I mentioned in the last letter. Without these invariants, we will often fall into "arguing merely about credibility."

These invariants will be something we can verify or test. For example, if someone asks for the temperature, we can give what the thermometer reads: "It is 85 degrees." That is an invariant, as opposed to saying, "It is warm" because the latter is ambiguous and different people will have different conceptions of what is warm and what isn't. But we can all agree on what the thermometer says. And we can verify it. If I say it's 80 degrees, you can look at the thermometer, too.

He also makes a distinction between *validity* and *truth*. The best way to remember this distinction is by way of example. Let's say I go shopping with twenty dollars in my pocket and I spend $12. I can make an assertion and say, "I have $8 left." Rapoport would say that if I check my arithmetic I am testing the *validity* of my assertion, but if I reach in my pocket and actually count the money then I am testing the *truth* of my assertion.

Thus, statements can be valid but not true. Jane is John's wife, so John is Jane's husband. A valid assertion as far it goes, but maybe it's not true; we can test it by some acceptable criteria—perhaps by examining legal documents, etc.

As for truth specifically, Rapoport's concept is more robust than what I've shown so far. He gives us a nice set of tests for the truth of an assertion. An assertion is operationally *true* if:

1. The assertion implies predictions to be tested by conceivable operations.
2. Operations have been carried out to test the predictions
3. The predictions have been verified by the operations.

If we fail at #3, then we say the assertion is *false*. If it fails #2, we say the assertion is *indeterminate*. And if it fails #1, we say it is *meaningless*. So here we have a neat way to talk about assertions. They are either true, false, indeterminate or meaningless.

The distinctions here are not sharp, as Rapoport admits, but they are a practical way to think through an assertion and give us a richer option than simply falling back on the old true/false dichotomy (constricted by the

Aristotelian Law of the Excluded Middle).

As usual, some examples will help explain these new labels...

Consider the statement: "If Hillary Clinton were president rather than Donald Trump in 2020, then fewer people would've died from COVID-19 in the United States."

That's a meaningless statement, from an OP perspective. There is no way to test such a statement for the simple reason that we cannot reconstruct the past. There is no way to go back in time and do it all over again but this time with Clinton as president. All such historical statements fail this test.

Statements such "God exists (or doesn't exist)" would fall in the same category because there is no conceivable test we could run to make a conclusion one way or the other. "God is love" or "Truth is beauty" and so on are all operationally meaningless. There is no way to test them. They might be meaningful in other symbolic ways, but at least via the OP lens, they are not.

If we say, "Tom is a good golfer," that statement as it stands doesn't mean anything unless we qualify by what we mean as "good." If it's something fairly objective, such as "He has a single-digit handicap" (indicating an objective scoring record of rounds played), then we could get past #1 and may have something.

Consider a statement about what it is like on a distant planet. We could make assertions about what it is like on some distant planet. And we could conceive of tests to verify our claims, but we have not, or cannot, actually perform such tests. In this case, we're past #1 but can't get by #2. Hence, we'd have to say such assertions are indeterminate. They might be true, but we can't tell, operationally, if they are.

Well, that's enough about OP. I like how it forces us to get at the meaning of any assertion. OP recognizes meaning lies in the experience of the person making the assertion. Therefore, to understand a person, we have to understand his or her experiences.

There is far more in Rapoport's books than what I've shared here, but it gives you a flavor. And we've added a couple of tools to your ever-expanding GS toolbox—the principle of non-additivity and operational philosophy's tests for assertions.

Your Fellow Time-Binder,

Chris

P.S. Wendell Johnson offered a set of three questions you can put to any proposition, in his book *Living with Change: The Semantics of Coping*:

- What do you mean?
- How do you know?
- What then?

The questions are simple, but they can be profound and revealing. The first tries to get people to think more carefully about what they are saying and offer links to the nonverbal world—things that you can see, taste, touch, etc. It is an attempt to gain clarity by bringing what is said into the world of examples and 'real' events, pushing back against mere verbalisms. The second question gets you to think of evidence—and weigh the quality and merit of such evidence. And the last question forces us to consider what consequences may come if such a statement is sound.

Combined, these questions bring a certain discipline against loose generalizations and errant time-binding. Try them out and see.

Letter 20

IFD Disease: Idealism, Frustration, and Demoralization

Dear Fellow Time-Binder,

Curious about Wendell Johnson? He is of the greats in the GS tradition. I've mentioned him more than a few times in these letters, so I understand your curiosity!

His writings are among my favorites in the GS realm. He made many contributions, including three wonderful books: *People in Quandaries: The Semantics of Personal Adjustment* (1946), *Your Most Enchanted Listener* (1956), and *Living with Change: The Semantics of Coping* (1972, published after his death from transcripts of talks). He also created a useful formulation of an idea that is uniquely associated with him. We'll get to that below. But first, more about the man.

Wendell "Jack" Johnson was born in 1906 on a Kansas farm. He was known as Jack to friends and close associates, because of his skill as a boxer (a trade he did not pursue), and Jack Johnson was the reigning heavyweight of his youth. Wendell Johnson had a stutter, and he would go on to attend the University of Iowa because they had a speech therapy clinic (one of the first). He attained his undergraduate, master's, and doctorate degrees at Iowa. His master's thesis, titled *Because I Stutter*, was published commercially.

Johnson himself became a speech pathologist because, as he often said, he needed one. He contributed much to this field and to the University of Iowa, so much so that the university would come to name their Speech and Hearing Center after Johnson.

Johnson "discovered" Korzybski in 1936. At this point, Johnson still stuttered badly. And by his own account, he had read everything in the literature about the condition attempting to find a cure. He even learned to play a fair game of ping-pong left-handed in an attempt to "re-wire" his brain. Nothing seemed to work.

A friend gave him a copy of *Science & Sanity* to review. The next day, he had an emergency appendectomy, and while laid up with that, he read *S&S*. Here is Johnson in his own words describing his experience reading the book:

The first two hundred pages were the strangest I've ever read. I put it aside, but something haunted me about the book. I had by this time taken a doctor's degree in clinical psychology and speech pathology and had worked five years in a speech clinic. Most of this time I had concentrated on the problem of stuttering. There was something new in the point of view of this book that changed my views on stuttering. I finished *Science and Sanity*, and I've never been the same since.

In 1938, he attended one of Korzybski's seminars. He was hooked ever after, and GS changed the way he thought about himself and the problem of stuttering. He began to work these ideas into his treatment, which led to influential innovations in the field at the time.

He wrote those two great books on GS and contributed countless lectures teaching it. In 1939, he introduced a course on general semantics at the University of Iowa. It was the first such course offered at an American University. According to Luther Sies, an associate who met Johnson in 1950, Johnson was a great speaker, and students crowded into his general semantics course. They came from all departments of the university. Sies estimates there were usually 120 attending his classes.

Sies ranks Johnson's influence on par with Hayakawa's, writing that they both "have probably done more to apply and communicate Korzybski's ideas than have anyone else." High praise indeed.

He died of a heart ailment in 1965, one year short of his 60th birthday. Johnson seemed well loved by colleagues and students alike. His death inspired much comment, including an obituary in *Time* magazine. He was also another exemplar in the conduct of his own life. As he put it: "One has to teach by example. General semantics is a course about thinking. There is an acid test for a teacher to try to teach by example—set an example of a kind of thinking—a kind of thinking that is extremely effective."

Joseph Stewart, who met Johnson in 1956, remarked in appreciation: "He appeared truly to live one of the sentences from his *Your Most Enchanted Listener*: 'All roads of wonder lead, with much meandering, to the Rome of self-fulfillment, a city within a city within a city without end.'"

Johnson's book *People in Quandaries* is still in print and serves as an excellent, and elegantly written, exposition of GS ideas. The first chapter, "Verbal Cocoons," is worth the price of admission by itself. In fact, it was published separately under the title "People in Quandaries" in *ETC* back in 1942.

Johnson maintains that many of our quandaries are verbal cocoons in which we encase ourselves. Society has a way of creating ideals to strive for.

These could include ways to dress, things to own, and activities to pursue. Advertising, movies, and social media can all awaken desires and lure you to 'need' things you never knew you needed. These feelings are probably as old as mankind itself. Socrates once said, after looking over luxury articles for sale in a market, "How many things there are I do not need."

But not everyone can be as detached as Socrates. And so we get sucked in the game and seed our own unhappiness. Schopenhauer wrote wonderfully about how we will never find contentment if we do not moderate our desires. Otherwise, they grow unchecked, never finally fulfilled. Wealth is like seawater, Schopenhauer wrote, "the more we drink of it, the thirstier we become." But what is 'wealth' really?

This is old wisdom. Checking desires, wants, goals, etc. lead to greater contentment with what we already have. And even with regards to what we have, it's still sound advice to hold on lightly to these externals. The inner life is all we have that is really ours, resistant to the grasping fingers of fate. The uncertain winds of fortune may blow our physical possessions and body this way and that, but a wise person will find solace within.

We can wonder about 'success' too, something our society puts much emphasis on. But what does 'success' mean? It is hard to define. As Johnson writes, "when 'success' cannot with certainty be claimed, 'failure' cannot with confidence be disavowed."

And here bubble up problems—feelings of frustration, inadequacy, unhappiness. . . Johnson believed in the therapeutic power of GS. Johnson thought a good part of these negative feelings grew out of ill-founded ideals—setting our aspirations and goals that we are quite unlikely to achieve.

The list of misevaluations is long: To want what you can't have; to want to change what you can't change; to want to do what you cannot do; to persistently demand something of yourself that you cannot accomplish; to set up standards that you cannot meet, etc.

A feeling of failure comes from a gap in what you expected, or wished for, and what you wound up with. In this way, 'failure' is a matter of evaluation. It is something for which you can exercise some control. If you allow yourself to assume unrealizable ideals, then you will eventually feel frustrated and finally demoralized.

Johnson gave this progression a name: IFD disease—from idealism to frustration to demoralization. He believed it was of epidemic proportions and that none of us truly escape its grasp. But the good news is that IFD has its roots in the semantic structures we use and adopt. These semantic structures can be changed. That's what GS is all about. And Johnson's book is an attempt to show us how we can work ourselves free of our verbal cocoons. "It is as though mankind had spun an enormous web of words—and caught itself," he wrote. "Our problem is, in large degree, one of unraveling this net of symbolism in which our human destiny has become entangled."

The idea of IFD caught on and has been widely cited in the GS literature. It has its roots in Korzybski, who formulated something similar in *S&S:*

> In life, numerous serious 'hurts' occur precisely because we do not appreciate some natural shortcomings and expect *too much*. Expecting too much leads to very harmful semantic shocks, disappointments, suspicions, fears, hopelessness, helplessness, pessimism, etc.

You may object and say there is nothing wrong with having big goals and lofty ambitions. You are free to think what you wish, of course. But I would simply remind you that highly ambitious goals that you are unlikely to ever attain will, by definition, not be fulfilled most of the time. And repeatedly setting goals that you do not reach is bound to lead to disappointment and frustration. You may not like it, but there it is.

And if you don't like it, I would ask you to think deeply about why you don't like it. Is it because self-help programs and commercials and Hollywood stars have implanted this idea that you need to "reach for the stars" and other such clichés? And besides, having low expectations doesn't mean you can't achieve. One of the richest men in the world, Charlie Munger (Warren Buffett's right-hand man at Berkshire Hathaway) said: "The first rule of a happy life is low expectations. If you have unrealistic expectations, you're going to be miserable all your life."

But what is 'happiness'? What does it mean to say you are happy? Perhaps we can invert and think of things destined to make us unhappy.

Paul Watzlawick's *The Situation is Hopeless But Not Serious: The Pursuit of Unhappiness* catalogs several ways in which we create unhappiness by adopting unrealizable ideals that have become widely (and unthinkingly) accepted, almost as a matter of course. For example, "to thine own self be true" seems a bit of wisdom most would agree with. But as Watzlawick writes, one who adopts this point of view is less likely to make compromises and most certainly will not make them happily. "Having to choose between the way the world *is* and the way he knows it *should be...* he will undauntedly opt for the latter and indignantly reject the former."

Choose your path wisely.

I would also say that Korzybski's thought here is entirely in line with the greater effort of GS: that is, to better match up our maps with the territory. Or, to put it another way, to create a better map, in the sense that it more accurately describes what happens to us. Crafting reasonable, attainable goals seems more like the work of a sane, well-adjusted person.

As Bob Pula put it, "Korzybski's work may be seen as a giant prescription for relieving the language-derived ills of humankind." Korzybski had his own prescription, related to IFD. In GS circles, we call it "Korzybski's Happiness Formula":

$$H = ME + MM$$

Happiness (H) equals minimum expectations (ME) plus maximum motivation (MM). Happiness in the Korzybskian sense doesn't mean unalloyed bliss; it means an extensionally grounded orientation. ME doesn't mean lowest possible; it means a realistic assessment of what you can do at the data you formulate your expectations. MM means what it says; that you're motivated as much as you can be. Think of what motivation entails: it means you're interested, engaged, willing, focused, etc. These are things associated with 'happy' people. Conversely, being disinterested, bored, unfocused, unwilling, etc. are not.

So, if you marry ME and MM, and you will be happy in the sense that you will, more often than not, get results that exceed, or at least are in line with, what your expectations and the effort you put into realizing them.

In this way, we might avoid unnecessary suffering. If all this has something of a Buddhist ring to it, you are not alone in making such an association. Many others have seen a similarity between GS and Zen Buddhism.

For example in an article in *ETC* (Autumn, 1951), Charles Morris—author of several books in the 1930 and 1940s—starts off with the following quote: "We generally think that 'A is A' is absolute, and that the proposition 'A is not-A' or 'A is B' is unthinkable. We have never been able to break through these conditions of the understanding ; they have been too imposing. But. . . words are words and no more. When words cease to correspond with facts it is time for us to part with words and return to facts."

Reading that, you'd think it came from Korzybski, but here is where Morris pulls his neat trick. It's not Korzybski. It's actually D.T. Suzuki, from his *Introduction to Zen Buddhism*. Morris goes on to note the many ways in which the concerns of Korzybski and Suzuki (and GS and Zen) overlap—in seeing the weaknesses of conceptualization; the limitations of language; the need to be master of our symbols rather than being mastered by them; and the common belief that such attitudes toward symbol making releases human spontaneity, wholeness, and sanity.

Of course, there are many differences as well. We do not want to overstate the case. Nonetheless, the similarities are quite striking. Corey Anton, a long-time GS teacher and author, sums up the two in a way that is particularly relevant to this letter:

> Arguably, general semantics might be understood as a fully Western scientific form of Zen Buddhism. Because we routinely bring unnecessary suffering to our lives due to forms of attachment and because we cling to expectations by verbally constructed ideas of how we think everything ought to be, GS offers a remedy for the agony of "reality" not living up to what we had hoped.

I love this aspect of GS—as a practical philosophy of everyday living, a toolkit to help make sense of what's going on around us and as a way of keeping sane and grounded and, yes, perhaps even happy.

Your Fellow Time-Binder,

Chris

Letter 21

Silence and the Delayed Reaction

Dear Fellow Time-Binder,

I'm pleased to hear you share my interest in this therapeutic vein of GS. We're not talking about a syrupy self-help program full of platitudes and slogans, but a sensible, rational, and workable set of principles that grow naturally out of GS itself.

With that, let's think about the power of silence and the delayed reaction, two other ideas you'll come across in the GS literature. We'll begin with an observation by Korzybski, which has long stuck by me ever since I first read it and which will put in motion the discussion to follow:

> The objective level is not words, and cannot be reached by words alone. We must point our finger and be silent, or we will never reach this level.

I don't love the word "objective" here. I'd rather say the "experiential" level; there is no such thing as an 'objective' world, as we discussed in the postscript on Rorty some letters back. Other times, Korzybski would call this level the "unsayable" level. What's unsayable? Wendell Johnson offered a neat way to get there. He said take a verbal description and try to define every term you used in the description. Then describe every word in your definition. When you start talking in circles, you've reached your set of undefined terms, your "unsayable" experiential level, for which you must be silent. We can only point and/or be silent.

This is, once again, old wisdom—especially in the East, where sages knew the unrivaled power of silence.

Bhagavan Sri Ramana Maharshi (1879–1950) epitomizes the power of silence. He lived almost his entire life around Arunachala, a sacred hill in southern India. He lived a simple life and was said to have only three possessions—his *kaupina* (a simple garment), his water pot, and his walking stick. Bhagavan exuded a sense of peace, contentment, and great presence. His simple teachings and humble personal example drew many to him. Eventually his followers built up an ashram around him, and people from all over the world and from all walks of life would come just for the privilege of sitting with him and perhaps having their questions answered.

Bhagavan did not always answer questions, or talk very much. He was known as "the silent guru." He often said his most powerful teachings were conveyed in silence. However, he was not always silent, and there are books that record "talks"—really bits of conversation he had with devotees and others who visited with him.

In several of these talks, Bhagavan sometimes expresses ideas similar to Korzybski's. On one occasion Bhagavan remarked:

> How does speech arise? First there is abstract knowledge. Out of this arises the ego, which in turn gives rise to thought, and thought to the spoken word. So the word is the great-grandson of the original source.

In this passage, Bhagavan verbalizes a kind of structural differential to show how far removed our talking is from the world 'out there.'

While Bhagavan's teachings grow out of his personal experiences, they fit well within an older tradition of Indian philosophy called Advaita Vedanta. For many, Bhagavan is the embodiment of that ideal. We won't go into what Advaita is all about, but I want to note it here should you choose to explore deeper. My time studying Bhagavan's life and teachings has been enormously rewarding, so, naturally, I would encourage you to learn more. But for purposes of this letter, I want to share one more thing about this ancient wisdom, which appreciates the gap between words and experience—indeed, which goes as far as Korzybski in saying that there are experiences and ideas unreachable by words.

Author John Allen Grimes has several wonderful examples in his book titled *Ramana Maharshi: The Crown Jewel of Advaita*. He points out that when Gautama the Buddha was asked "What is the truth?" he remained silent. When Pilate asked Jesus the same question, Jesus was also silent. And an Upanishadic sage named Vaskalin, when asked the same question by a seeker named Bhava, he, too, remained silent.

There are other examples I can think of from my own reading. "Let thy speech be better than silence or else be silent," says the sage Pseudo-Dionysius the Areopagite (who lived in the late 5th and early 6th centuries). Søren Kierkegaard urges us to consider the "lily of the field and the bird of the air," and suggests our troubles are amplified by our talk. And of course there is Wittgenstein: "Whereof one cannot speak, thereof one must be silent."

All these traditions and sages point to silence as having some unappreciated value, beyond what words can convey.

In the GS tradition, a number of teachers have tried to create an inner silence through various techniques. Wendell Johnson, for example, put forth the idea of making it a game—you would pick up, say, a pencil and just try to feel the sensations of holding the pencil without letting words come into play. When words did arrive, you were to drop the pencil. The game, then, is to see how long you can hold on to the pencil.

Harry Weinberg offered similar techniques. One involved food. You were to concentrate on your food and really taste it, even close your eyes and savor the textures and flavor and aromas. The idea is to try to slow down the verbalizations and to reach that silent level. Meditation is another way people try to reach this level, where words cannot go.

How well these methods work is a matter I'll leave for your own discovery. But I believe it is worth some effort, even if unsuccessful, to try from time to time to check the flow of words. Try to access this different level of awareness, a more sensory and unstructured experience.

There is nothing mystical or magical about it. As Weinberg says, you are tapping into a world "only dimly experienced previously because they had been buried under a smothering blanket of words." The verbalizing we do exists for the sake of the nonverbal, silent level—not vice versa. And he goes on to say, this is why general semanticists tend to place a greater value on the nonverbal than the verbal. (Note: This is not to say words are not important. They are critical to time-binding, which in the GS worldview is the high art of being human. We are simply giving the unsayable its due.)

Hayakawa went so far as to say GS was "ultimately a non-verbal discipline. It is a discipline in silence, of dissolving away the encrusted verbalizations and abstractions, the dogmas and creeds that envelope most of us like layers of barnacles." Hayakawa wants us to look, listen, smell, feel—to *experience* the outside world, to develop "a sharper awareness of the world of not-words." We'll give him the final word here on silence:

> Against that sharper awareness, it will be possible for us to make somewhat more meaningful statements than we are accustomed to making. And having made them, we will not be satisfied with them, because we are always aware that the non-verbal realities (like the taste of strawberries) are ultimately not communicable.

Next, we must say a word or two about a related concept you'll come across in the GS literature: the delayed reaction.

We're not talking about delaying your reaction to the hot pan you just grabbed with your bare hand or your reaction to the dog that just ran in front of your car. For this reason, I prefer the term "delayed evaluation," because that's what we're really talking about here: a practice whereby you try to withhold judgment—*epoché*, as the ancient Greek skeptics called it—even if briefly, with an eye toward making better evaluations.

The whole of GS is basically geared toward getting you to slow down a bit. After all, if you're thinking about dating events and using indexes, etc., just by nature that process is going to force you to think a bit more than you would otherwise. Consciousness about abstracting means you'll be more attune to the gap between "map" and "territory," between "words" and the "world out there."

Hayakawa made a nice point about this in his book *Language in Action*. He wrote how learning to delay your evaluations is a mark of adulthood. But bad experiences, miseducation, outdated beliefs, propaganda and other influences can leave us all with "areas of insanity" or "areas of infantilism." So maybe you had a bad experience with a spider that bit you when you were kid and now are frightened of every spider you see. That would be a misevaluation. And it would take some work for you to get over the idea that every spider means a potential spider bite—to basically delay your evaluation.

Hayakawa points out how there are areas where we're "blind by prejudice" and can't "think straight." Again, it takes some work to figure out where these areas are for you personally. They will be different for everyone. And then you can consciously work on delaying your evaluation.

For example, I like to tell the story about a financial conference where I was a speaker. After my talk, a guy in overalls approached me. Overalls! At a financial conference! My immediate reaction was "country bumpkin who knows nothing, I gotta get out of this conversation." But he turned out to be a wealthy and smart man. If I had delayed my reaction, I might've been more intrigued about a man so self-assured and unconcerned about what other people would think, that he'd wear overalls to a financial conference. Moreover, I might've reflected on the fact that the conference was not cheap and he had to pay his way in like everybody else and the quality of attendees was by nature quite high, etc.

We carry all kinds of assumptions in our head about people that can lead us to make snap judgments and poor evaluations. GS—with the working devices, safety devices, and other techniques we've talked about in these letters—is an effort to get us to delay our evaluations... and think.

We can't do this all the time. Nobody is perfect. As Korzybski often said, "No one can always be conscious of abstracting and delay all his reactions, including me—and I wrote the book." But it's sort of like exercise, even some is better than none.

Your Fellow Time-Binder,

Chris

Letter 22

Logical Fate

Dear Fellow Time-Binder,

We spent a lot of time on words and getting at definitions and meanings. Throughout our letters, we've taken some care to build proper assumptions into our language about the world out there.

We want to get these foundational aspects of our thinking on sound footing, so that our reasoning, which flows from them, is useful. And here we get to the idea of Logical Fate, or Logical Destiny. (Pula didn't like the mystical sound of these terms and so coined "neuro-linguistic inevitability." I'll take the mystical sounding phrases, sorry Pula. There is something to be said for poetry, after all.) Stated simply, it means from certain premises certain conclusions necessarily follow. We'll consider this insight in more detail below.

Logical Fate is an idea Korzybski borrowed from his friend Cassius J. Keyser (1862–1947). Keyser taught at Columbia University and was a philosophically minded mathematician who wrote well and widely on a variety of issues. He's the author of over a dozen books on thinking and mathematics, as well as treatments of Charles Saunders Peirce, Benedict Spinoza, and Roger Bacon.

Korzybski sent Keyser the manuscript of *Manhood of Humanity* in 1920. Keyser later wrote that he began the book with "indifference and misgiving" but quickly became interested as he read. He concluded the book was one of "great originality, great power and great importance." (All this is in Kodish's biography of Korzybski.) They met later that year and seemed to hit it off and became lifelong friends.

Keyser would be an important source of inspiration and guidance for Korzybski. And Keyser learned, too, from Korzybski, and remained enthusiastic about his ideas. *Manhood of Humanity* included, as an appendix, a lengthy "lecture" (though actually made up of part of an address and part of an article) by Keyser titled "Korzybski's Concept of Man." Keyser remained an enthusiast of "that mighty process which Korzybski happily designates by the term Timebinding."

I must also share Keyser's poetic rendering of time-binding, from his work *Mathematical Philosophy:*

> If human being are by nature civilization-builders, or "time-binders," and if all time-binders, or civilization-builders, are both inheritors from the toil of bygone generations and trustees for the generations to come, then we humans stand in the double relationship—debtors of the dead, trustees of the unborn—thus uniting past, present and future in one living, growing reality.

In that book, too, Keyser formulated the idea of logical fate. Korzybski thought "the discovery of logical fate... its elaboration and formulation, is of such importance" that if the book has nothing else in it "the book would live forever."

Logical Fate begins with a simple observation: We have certain choices we make every day. And once we make those choices we are "bound by a destiny of consequences beyond the power of passion or will to control or modify." Another choice means another destiny and so it goes on and on. "The world of ideas is, you see, the empire of Fate," Keyser wrote.

Though his insight originated in mathematics—where you can readily see that certain postulates lead inexorably to certain conclusions—Keyser applied it more widely "to all manner of doctrinistic contentions of wise men, knaves, fanatics and fools," including Plato's *Republic*, Darwin's *Origin of the Species*, the Sermon on the Mount, and much more. (Keyser wasn't the first to make this move. For example, philosophers such as Descartes, Hobbes, and Spinoza had a fondness for geometrical reasoning because it seemed to build inexorably from certain initial assumptions. And they, too, tried to apply it to a wider area of knowledge.)

In an early paper, "Fate and Freedom" (1923), Korzybski took Keyser's idea, with ample reference to his friend's book, and incorporated them into an outline of his own theory of time-binding and his nascent discipline of GS (which was still in its early days and which he was calling "human engineering" at that point, a name he soon discarded).

In "Fate and Freedom," Korzyski pointed out how intellectual life is a process of abstractions, generalizations, and assumptions that manifest themselves in words. He noted how this ongoing process led to the creation of a number of propositions and doctrines—all inherently governed by logical fate. For this reason, it is very important that we examine the assumptions we use as the raw materials in formulating these doctrines. When people don't do this—and Korzybski thought the vast majority do not—they are liable to "take labels, creations of their own rational will for objects, and objects for events as true constituents of nature, and they fight and die for them."

Our freedom is not absolute, Korzybski wrote, "we are governed by logical fate." But we must start somewhere and that often begins with undefined terms or vague notions. The important thing was to go back and revise our base assumption, to have a process whereby we apply and revise what we learned in an endless cycle. "Human knowledge is inexhaustible," as he wrote. "No set is undefined absolutely, but only relatively so."

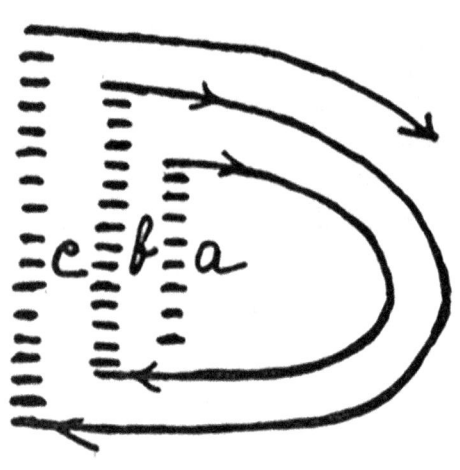

In S&S, he would sketch out this process in a diagram, reproduced nearby. Initial assumptions "a" are tested and revised into "b," which are tested and revised again to "c," and so on.

By the way, I love Korzybski's diagrams. They are low-tech and simple looking, but they also cohere somehow into a single Korzybskian art style. They're like hieroglyphics; they make no sense unless you have a certain Korzybskian key.

Anyway, Korzybski realized in practice, the process was far more complicated. And he emphasized the hidden metaphysics embedded in language, the silent postulates that imply theorems. "He who accepts uncritically the vocabulary made by X, accepts unwillingly and un-beknowingly X's metaphysics," he wrote. "This fact is of very great importance."

In his paper, "Fate and Freedom," Korzybski illustrated Logical Fate with a diagram, one that has ever since recurred in the GS literature: (See diagram on next page.)

I am not fond of it, I must admit. And you can probably guess why by now. I choke on the word "truer." We would be better served by letting our guide be usefulness (as we've broadly considered it in these letters), not 'truth' (which is problematic). Accepting the word 'truth' here would be an example of using a word and adopting a metaphysic that goes along with it. Nothing is lost here by simply swapping out the word "truer" and replacing it with "more useful." Actually, what we lose is, perhaps, a dogmatic sense of certitude that comes with accepting the idea we've found a "truth."

Beyond this objection, there is another: In life, errant assumptions can still lead to useful propositions. Hans Vaihinger wrote a whole book about this called *The Philosophy of 'As If.'* His theory of fictionalism runs as follows:

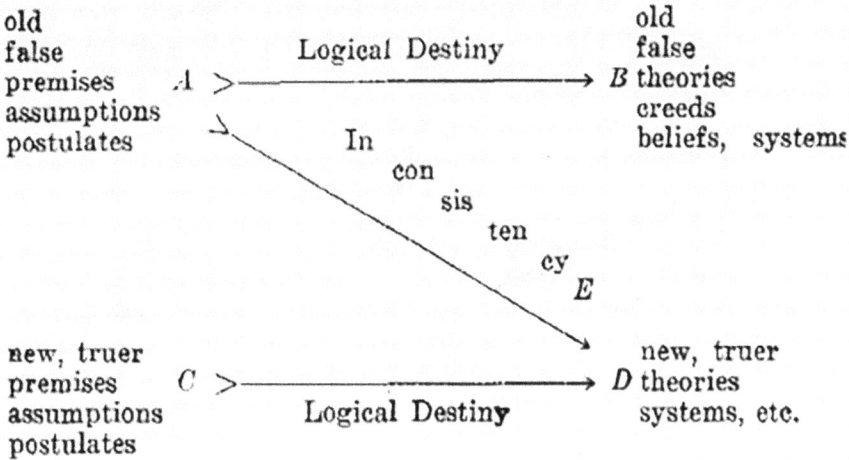

"An idea whose theoretical untruth or incorrectness, and therewith its falsity, is admitted, is not for that reason practically valueless and useless; for such an idea, in spite of its theoretical nullity[,] may have great practical importance."

He was not the first to have such a thought—he admits Kant as an inspiration, but there is also Jeremy Bentham, as C.K. Ogden has written (*Bentham's Theory of Fictions*). The idea takes us far afield from GS, but perhaps the idea is not so radical on a simple level. We all have stories of being "right" for the "wrong reasons" or operating under a false theory to good effect, even if later we come to know our error. I am also reminded of the pragmatists, particularly William James and John Dewey, challenging our notions of "truth." (And in modern times, perhaps the epitome of this approach lies in Richard Rorty's work.)

Beyond this: self-deception is a well-known technique in the field of psychology. Google "benefits of self-deception," and you'll get a long list of studies and book reviews on the subject.

In sports, self-deception is widely taught. For example, golf coaches teach you to think you will make every putt; most people will sink more putts believing this obvious "untruth." In medicine, self-deception can improve your chances of getting well. In war, belief in the power of spells and charms can increase the performance of soldiers. And perhaps the best example of all is found in the sphere of religion, where humans have crafted intricate belief systems that bring a variety of benefits to believers.

But you may worry: If we ditch the concept of truth and adopt one of usefulness, as I have been saying in this letter, do we not create problems of another sort, such as an inability to combat lies because they are "useful" from some point of view?

I don't think so. Part of the answer may lie in a preposition: *a* truth seems an improvement over truth unadorned or, worse, *the* truth. The latter two strongly imply categorical Aristotelian thinking; "*a* truth" describes an open-ended possibility of other 'truths.' But why go halfway? Truth itself is an Aristotelian category, and like EMA, we can get by without it.

In any event, Logical Fate is a useful tool in the GS toolkit, as it reminds us to carefully consider our assumptions. If we want to change our behavior, or influence the behavior of others, we can start with the underlying assumptions such behavior entails. The Keyser-Korzybski formulation, as Pula once called it, reminds us of the unbreakable link between premises and conclusions.

Your Fellow Time-Binder,

Chris

Letter 23

How to Ask a Question

Dear Fellow Time-Binder,

Have you ever heard of the Lapidus Principle? You probably have, you just don't know it by that name. Stuart Mayper, another GS teacher, wrote a story to show the principle and how it got its name.

To paraphrase: Sam Lapidus (La-peed-us) was on a train with his friend Garfunkel. They were not worldly people. And they were not accustomed to the luxury of a railroad dining car. About two-thirds through their meal, the waiter brings them each a bowl of warm water with a few rose-petals floating on the surface and a slice of lemon on the side.

Not knowing what to make of it, Sam and Garfunkel wonder what it could be. Soup? Can't be soup. They already had soup. Dessert? But they didn't order dessert yet. Can't be that. Sam is too embarrassed to ask the waiter and tells Garfunkel they should just sit quietly and act like men of the world. But Garfunkel can't stand it any longer and asks what it is.

The waiter explains the bowl was there so that the diners may clean their fingers. After the waiter left, the two sat in silence for a bit. And finally Lapidus spoke, thus stating the Lapidus Principle: "You ask a foolish question, you'll get a foolish answer!"

Questions can be tricky. We want to take some care in formulating our questions, otherwise, as the Lapidus Principle states, we risk foolish answers. You can think of it as a variation on Logical Fate—once locked into a certain question, you may be led inexorably to certain conclusions, where different formulations inevitably lead to different answers.

Perhaps, then, it is not surprising that the architect of Logical Fate, the mathematician Cassius Keyser, should have something to say about the nature of questions: "It is often said that a fool can ask a question which a wise man cannot answer. It is better to say that a wise man can answer questions which a fool cannot ask."

Keyser meant that it is not easy to ask a "good" question. It is easy to ask a pseudo-question. As a result, we spend a lot of time going round and round on questions for which there are no meaningful or useful answers.

Wendell Johnson was another stickler about asking questions. Johnson probably thought more about questions than any GS teacher. His test for any question was to ask the following: "What does the question mean on the level of non-words, on the level of observation and experience? That is, precisely what factual observations might I or anyone else make in order to answer it?" (*Your Most Enchanted Listener*).

Tough bird, that Johnson. Most questions dissolve into a puddle of unanswerable nothingness after applying his acid test...

Look at these questions with Johnson's acid test in mind:

> When did time begin?
> Did we invent math or did we discover it?
> Where does a thought go when it's forgotten?
> Do we have free will or is everything predestined?
> Is there life after death?
> Is it really possible to experience anything objectively?
> What are dreams?
> What is the goal of humanity?
>
> (Source: https://icebreakerideas.com/unanswerable-questions)

Do any of them meet Johnson's requirements? I don't think so.

Now, this doesn't mean GS practitioners can't ask speculative or fun questions. We simply recognize them as such. We don't take the answers all that seriously. No general semanticist ever got upset over answers to the question "Is there life after death?"

Pula used a simple typology to help sort these things out. Questions are either operational/extensional, speculative, fun or pathology-inducing/intensional. This typology is not exhaustive, but it's a handy way to think about questions.

Operation/extensional: These are questions where answers are readily found. What is your home address? How do you get to Monticello from here? How do you make cornbread? How long will it take me to read *War & Peace*? The common element here is that we can do something to get an answer. We look up addresses and consult maps; we can look at recipes; and we can keep track of how long it takes to read a book.

Speculative: These are questions that may not have answers yet, but for which we think we can eventually get answers. Pula says a good speculative question is one that becomes, at some point, operational/extensional. So, in early 2020, we didn't know what a COVID vaccine would look like or what effects it might have. To ask the question was speculative, but it was one that we could answer over time as vaccines were developed. Most scientific inquiry falls in the speculative realm; we ask questions we can't answer just now, but we have means to go about finding answers. Or the passage of time may answer it. Who will be the next president of the United States? Seems a fair speculative question. We can talk about it, and eventually we will know.

Fun: Who would win in a fight Superman or Batman? Who is the greatest golfer of all time? What uniform looks best? Which novel is better? These are fun questions. There are no right or wrong answers. The answers are not to be taken seriously. Pula says these may be the healthiest of all questions, because "they generate little negative tension (except, perhaps, in those who don't want to play)."

Pathology-inducing/intensional: These are the unanswerable questions of the world. The "why me?" questions. The "why is the world against me" questions. These lie, in Pula's words, at the "gateway of 'paranoia' and the various 'schizophrenias.'"

"Why are things the way they are?" is another specimen—but sometimes you can give a clever answer. Edmund Carpenter tells the story of when Knud Rasmussen, an ethnologist, asked an Inuit hunter named Aua why life was as it was.

Aua seemed a budding general semanticist, because he did not take the bait and verbalize an answer. Instead, Aua took Rasmussen outside and pointed—at the hunters returning empty-handed after long hours on the ice. And Aua asked Rasmuusen "Why?" Then Aua took him to an igloo where hungry children shivered, pointed and asked "Why?" and then to another, where a hard-working and well-meaning woman lay miserably ill—and again he asked Rasmussen "Why?"

There is no answer one can put in words why life is as it is. "We explain nothing," Aua finally said, "but in what I have just shown you lies our answer to all you ask." Many things just *are* and defy verbal explanations.

A clear sign of a potentially pathology-inducing question is one that aims for certainty where certainty is not available. Wendell Johnson thought many of our troubles come from this quest for certainty, "a preoccupation with unanswerable questions, questions asked in absolute terms about a world of relative 'facts'—a concern for neat and last-word statements about a reality of continuous process" (*Living with Change*).

He goes on to say:

> "But I think it is not good for us or anyone to read writers or hear speakers who pretend they know things. For then we end up with the notion that there are final answers and that it is desirable to know them. Well, this is a disease. This is delusional. We do not know anything for

sure. We don't know anything completely. We just keep trying to find out. And we try to do a little better every day. But it is the difference between thinking we are done and knowing that we never will be that is important." (*Living with Change*)

Besides, as Johnson says, there is something quite liberating in the idea that some questions are unanswerable. The willingness to leave certain pathological questions alone also fosters clear-headedness by not allowing you to fall for alluring nonsense.

In addition to the Pula typology, I have a category I call "Too hard." The inspiration comes from Charlie Munger, the long-time business partner of Warren Buffett and vice chairman at Berkshire Hathaway. Munger coined the phrase "too hard pile" for investing ideas where it would be too difficult and require too much work to know if they were good ideas or bad ideas. The usefulness of a "too hard pile" is as a time saver; it helps you focus your attention on matters where you'll likely get a greater reward.

So, for me, a question such as "what is the value of education?" seems "too hard." I have to think about what we mean by 'education.' Literacy? Math skills? Formal education? College degree? What exactly? After that, I have to think about 'value.' Measured how? By earnings power? Or by internal feelings of satisfaction? Or what? Both 'value' and 'education' are problematic and vague. Thinking of Johnson's acid test, what factual observations might I or anyone else make in order to answer it? The question, at a minimum, needs a lot of work. And I'm not sure the answer would be worth much anyway.

We can lean on operational philosophy too. We can try to cast our questions in operational terms. (See our earlier letter, #17, on Rapoport and his operational philosophy.) Maybe we ditch the whole question entirely.

Johnson offered a practical way to recast questions. He said to rephrase the question to an *if so, what then* form. So, instead of asking, "Should we raise the minimum wage?" we could rephrase the question and say, "If we raised the minimum wage, what then?" This gets away from the problematic *should* and instead focuses our attention on making observations that we can organize and test.

If you say, "There isn't anything I can observe to answer what I want to know" then Johnson suggests you "need to go off in some quiet spot and ask yourself where does that leave you."

Johnson says such questions are unanswerable and stir up unresolvable disagreement. There can be terrible consequences to trying to answer unanswerable questions. I recall the religious conflicts of the Reformation era. The bitter feuds and bloodshed over unanswerable theological questions—over sacraments and biblical interpretations, etc.

Asking proper questions would probably avoid a lot of arguments. I recall an amusing anecdote told by a teacher, Rebekah Baron, in a letter to *ETC*. She had her high schoolers thinking about how we use words in different ways. Baron wanted her students to pay attention to any arguments they were having, or other people were having, and see if clarifying strategies akin to those suggested here might resolve disputes, or at least expose how word use might be the heart of a dispute. She wanted her students to ask "What do you mean by..."

Baron reported, in her letter, five different episodes where her students helped resolve arguments or misunderstandings by helping to clarify the meaning of different words using the GS tools she had taught them.

But there was a funny ending to her letter. "Incidentally," Baron wrote, "it was discovered that not all people like to have their disagreements settled. One student reported that people 'resented her interfering in their argument' and told her to mind her own business."

Your Fellow Time-Binder,

Chris

Letter 24
The General Principle of Uncertainty

Dear Fellow Time-Binder,

I agree when you say that underlying GS is the idea that we don't know as much as we think we do. Uncertainty is built into the system. Think about the early letters we exchanged, establishing the world as process (always changing) and how no two events are exactly alike and how we never know all the details. Uncertainty flows naturally from these assumptions. Reject uncertainty, and you reject these assumptions.

Korzybski understood the implications of these initial assumptions. In *S&S*, he wrote how the uniqueness of all events means "all statements about them are only probable in various degrees, introducing a *general principle of uncertainty* in *all statements*" [italics in the original].

Pula thought the idea important enough that he gave "general uncertainty" its own entry in his *A General-Semantics Glossary*. Pula wrote well about this topic—and even created something called the Uncertainty Umbrella, which we'll get to—so this would be a good time to introduce you to this exemplary GS teacher, one of my favorites.

Robert Paul Pula (1928–2004) was born in Baltimore, where he was a lifelong resident. He graduated from Loyola College and started his career as a counselor to soldiers. Later he taught English and communication at various city schools and community colleges.

He was quite fond of his Polish ancestry and interested in Polish culture, which comes through in writings as well with his ample mentions of Polish thinkers such as Tarski, Lukasiewicz Skolimowski, and others. His interest in Polish thinkers led him to Korzybski. Pula was a member of the Polish Heritage Association of Maryland (and editor of its journal), served as president of the Polish Student Association, director of the Polonia Chorus, and a member of the Polish Legion of American Veterans.

He was a graduate of Loyola College and began his teaching career as a counselor to college-bound soldiers at Forts Meade and Holabird. He later taught English and communication at city schools and community colleges. He even married a woman of Polish descent, Irene Jaroszewski, in 1955, whom he had met through the Polish Students Association.

He was also a musician and composer. He wrote his first piano composition when he was 14 and performed in city gatherings, particularly at Polish cultural events. He also enjoyed painting and cartooning.

On top of all this, he was a great enthusiast of Korzybski's. (He was working on a biography, but died before he completed it.) He was the lead lecturer at the Institute for some thirty years, edited the *Bulletin* from 1977 to 1985, and was director of the Institute from 1983 to 1986. He wrote the preface to the 5th edition of *Science & Sanity*—an 8-page tour de force that highlighted 31 Korzybskian formulations Pula considered original.

Whew, not only do GS people often have a great sense of humor, but they're often polymaths. Pula seemed a person of great energy and quite a character. I always enjoy coming across Pula anecdotes in my GS reading.

For example, Susan Presby Kodish remembered how he would host "Pula's Pub" after seminars in his room until 2 a.m. or so each night. Even so, "he started each class with sharp, follow-up GS-related comments on what he had observed since his last class. His unique combination of seriousness, wit and whimsy endeared him to me."

She fondly remembers road trips with Pula to the New York area for Institute meetings and events. "Bob took great delight in the New Jersey Turnpike and our stops along the way," she remembered. "Let him at that hamburger and fries; he was one happy man."

Some of his lectures survive on YouTube. I've enjoyed listening to these and now when I read his works, I have his voice in my head. In addition to the *Glossary*, Pula wrote many articles and papers. His annotated bibliography, by Pula himself, includes 106 items.

Bruce Kodish (Korzybski's biographer and the husband of the aforementioned Susan, with who he co-authored an introductory GS book titled *Driving Yourself Sane*) speculated that Pula's Roman Catholic upbringing and education in Thomistic philosophy at a Jesuit college helped him appreciate how radical Korzybski's insights were. Pula converted from the dogmatic teachings of the church to "a dedicated uncertaintist—what he called a 'born-again agnostic.'"

Pula did talk about this point in a 2000 lecture. He said that when he first read Korzybski his only reaction was "Oh, pooh, pooh, pooh, pooh." He goes on to say: "And I admitted to myself that if this guy. . . didn't have the name 'Korzybski,' I'd probably throw the book into the fire, but I felt obliged because I'm also a student of Polish stuff, culture, etc., so I insisted that I keep reading. And finally I got the neuro-linguistic point, in the Introduction."

A kind of revelation soon followed: "If this guy is right, then almost everybody else that I've read up to this point is wrong." And so began his long engagement with Korzybski and GS...

In that long engagement, he wrote perceptively and forcefully about Korzybski's GS—including its inherent principle of uncertainty, which is the subject of our letter. In a paper titled, "Knowledge, Uncertainty and Courage: Heisenberg and Korzybski," he explored Korzybski's idea that uncertainty was an inescapable part of the abstracting process.

I'm sure you've heard of Werner Heisenberg. What has become known as the "Heisenberg Uncertainty Principle" covers a lot more ground than his initial idea, though it was still a blockbuster idea in the world of physics. Basically, Heisenberg posited that you could not measure with accuracy certain pairs of physical qualities, such as velocity and position, at the same time. The greater the accuracy of your measurement of velocity, the less accurate your measure of position, and vice versa.

This idea made quite the splash at the time and many, including Einstein, resisted it or refused to accept it altogether. Korzybski embraced it. In fact, Heisenberg was one of the people to whom Korzybski dedicated *S&S* —or more specifically, as Korzybski wrote, his dedication covered the works of the dedicatees which had "greatly influenced my enquiry." Korzybski used a handful of quotes sprinkled throughout *S&S* as chapter heads and refers to Heisenberg numerous other times.

Why did Korzybski embrace Heisenberg? Partly because, as Pula says, Korzybski had "formulational nerve," "epistemological guts," and, more simply, "courage." Probably more importantly was that uncertainty sits at the root of the GS system—the rejection of absolute sameness in all aspects, a thing we never encounter in the 'real' world.

Korzybski had these ideas well before Heisenberg. In the 1920s, he was already writing about how the accuracy of our statements and descriptions are limited, or conditioned, by the symbols we use. They cannot represent the world 'out there' with certain accuracy—because we live in a world where everything is constantly changing, where not two things are exactly alike, where we can't know all the details, etc.

Korzybski's most forceful and often quoted statement of general uncertainty is: "Whatever you say something is, it is not." Quite profound once you mull over it. Whatever you say something 'is,' will be too limiting. That something will be more than you say, because your description will always leave details out, besides there will be things about it that you cannot capture in words (think back to the 'unsayable' level). And that thing is ever changing, even if only slightly. These are some of the reasons why whatever you say something is, it is not.

Thus, uncertainty. We make all of our statements and descriptions probabilistically. As Pula is careful to point out, this doesn't mean we can't make relatively secure statements. Using Korzybski's devices—the date, the index, the etc., the hyphen, the quotes—we can make some fairly secure extensional statements. And those devices strongly imply such statements will be subject to future revision, if required. But we can make confident statements within the confines of GS. As Pula put it, "Loss of certainty does not imply the impossibility of confidence."

Ironically, our statements become even more secure when we adapt probability because our statements, over the long run, become more likely to "hit their mark"—i.e., accurately match up with what happens in the nonverbal world.

Pula wrote that it was the certaintist that had the most insecure formulations because the certaintist would constantly be struck with unexpected events. "Nervous systems do not take well to such repeated structural mismatches/insults," Pula wrote. He summarized the implications of general uncertainty with a drawing he sometimes used in seminars. It's called "The Uncertainty Umbrella." As with Korzybski's drawings, Pula's too has a certain charm in its crudeness and hieroglyphic quality. I've included it below. Have a look.

If you think of an umbrella as keeping you dry when it's raining, you will get the gist of his insight. We're pelted with uncertainty—the process world, things changing, or as Pula put it "change thinging," etc. But our ability to deal with uncertainty using our GS tools allows us a certain logical precision. We know maps do not equal territories (M ≠ T). And this is a great asset in life, on the job, etc.

I note that some people do not react well to being told "nothing is certain."

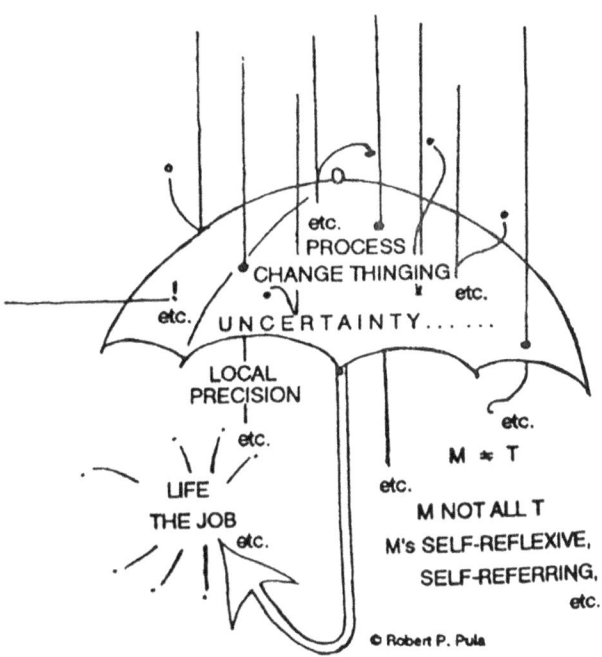

The Uncertainty Umbrella

(Please note, as Pula did, that "certainty" is a multiordinal term—and so, being certain about uncertainty leads to very different conclusions (and behaviors) than being certain about certainty.")

I am not one of those people. I revel and delight in uncertainty. To me it's exhilarating to grasp the idea that so many explanations may yet be possible, that so much of the world is yet unknown and that so many outcomes may yet emerge. To me, living in a world with certainty would be a bummer; it would seem lifeless by comparison, boring, unthinking, unchanging, etc. Uncertainty makes life interesting. . . and acceptance makes one more tolerant.

A lot of bigotry and hatred and bitter political divisions seem unlikely if we all embraced general uncertainty as a matter of course. Uncertainty entails letting doubt shine its light in the closet of your mind. Think how different debates about abortion, borders, taxes, international relations, war, etc. would be if you could not make certain statements about any them? If instead you cast all your ideas in terms of probability—English minus the absolutes, using dates and indexes, etc. I fail to see how such a world wouldn't be more tolerant, less violent, more creative and sharper in its thinking.

On this point, Pula in his paper on uncertainty quoted Jacob Bronowski who called the principle of uncertainty "the Principle of Tolerance." He noted the irony about the Heisenberg principle, from which the modern principle of uncertainty draws strength that at the "very time when this was being worked out there should rise, under Hitler in Germany and other tyrants elsewhere, a counter-conception: a principle of monstrous certainty."

In any event, we do seem to live in a world operating under the principles of general uncertainty—as we noted at the start of our letter. And so, 'better' time-binding would demand we take account of it in our descriptions, statements, explanations, etc. Pula suggested we need the courage to see, as Korzybski did, that most of our problems seem to stem "not from uncertainty but from mistaken certainty wrongly applied."

Your Fellow Time-Binder,

Chris

Letter 25

The Sapir-Whorf Hypothesis

Dear Fellow Time-Binder,

Yes, I think Pula is a lot of fun to read. I wish someone had collected more of his stuff and published it in book form. Maybe someday! Another one of his papers I like has to do with the Sapir-Whorf hypothesis, where he connects Korzybski to Nietzsche.

Which reminds me, we should probably cover the Sapir-Whorf hypothesis—which sort of lurks in the background of GS. Korzybski liked the idea. And it is an interesting hypothesis. So what is it?

Well, it's named after an American anthropologist/linguist Edward Sapir (1884–1939) and his student Benjamin Lee Whorf (1897–1941). Our focus for the moment will be on Whorf, who developed ideas he initially found in Sapir's work.

Whorf was educated as a chemical engineer at MIT and after graduation worked at a firm as a fire prevention engineer. He seemed quite good at it, and his advice was sought after by chemical manufacturers, according to John Carroll (who edited a collection of Whorf's work, after Whorf's death at the age of 44). This fire prevention work would come into play later in developing his hypothesis.

Whorf also had an interest in linguistics, which he took up in 1924 as an amateur. He was curious Mayan hieroglyphics, as well as the languages of the Aztecs and Hopi, among other linguistic interests. He took a trip to Mexico in 1930, filling notebooks with observations.

He first met Sapir in 1928. But the really close contact began when Sapir came to the University of Chicago in 1931 to teach a class on linguistics. Whorf enrolled. His interaction with Sapir supercharged Whorf's development and by the fall of 1937, Whorf was lecturing at Yale.

Sapir died in 1939, and Whorf's health was also in decline. In the last couple of years of his life, Whorf developed his idea of linguistic relativity, which became the Sapir-Whorf hypothesis. His definitive presentation of the idea is in his 1939 memorial article for Sapir, titled "The Relation of Habitual Thought And Behavior to Language."

Whorf begins his paper with a quotation from Sapir, which reads, in part:

> Human beings do not live in the objective world alone, nor alone in the world of social activity as ordinarily understood, but are very much at the mercy of the particular language which has become the medium of expression for their society... We see and hear and otherwise experience very largely as we do because the language habits of our community predispose certain choices of interpretation.

In a nutshell, the Sapir-Whorf hypothesis says that the language you use influences, even dictates, what kinds of observations and evaluations you can make.

Whorf drew on his experience as a fire prevention engineer. He noticed how people who take great care around the storage of "gasoline drums." But care greatly diminishes when people say the drums are "empty gasoline drums," even though 'empty' drums are perhaps the more dangerous as they still contain explosive vapors that can ignite on, say, a carelessly tossed cigarette stub.

Whorf zeros in on the word 'empty' and our linguistic conditioning for that word to mean "null and void, negative, inert" which gets us into trouble when dealing with gases. Whorf gives another example using "limestone." Because it contains the word "stone," people tend to equate "stone" with "non-combustible." In fact, limestone burns vigorously.

Another example involves a kettle of boiling varnish, which a worker realized was close to the temperature at which it would ignite. So, he took it off the fire and moved it some distance away. Here Whorf points to the idea that the kettle is "off" the fire and therefore will not continue to heat. But the internal process of convection from the intensity of the heated kettle continued even when "off" the fire. The varnish ignited.

One more: A tannery discharged wastewater in a settling basin, partly roofed. Such a basin would commonly be called a "pool of water." A worker threw a match in the water to put it out... but the decomposing waste matter emitted a gas, partially trapped under the wood roof, which was flammable. Hence, the match lit a column of flame, which spread to the adjoining building. Again, Whorf cites the linguistic root of the behavior in thinking of the liquid in the basin as "water" and hence "not flammable."

There are more examples in his paper, and even more examples Whorf says he could've cited. But suffice to say, it shows what he's aiming at: certain behaviors derive from "the linguistic formula in which the situation is spoken of... analyzed, classified and allotted its place in the world."

This extends far beyond single words and phrases. It encompasses all grammatical categories—plurality, gender, classifications (animate, inanimate, etc.), tenses, voices and more. There is much more to Whorf's paper, but we will stop here as I hope you have the gist of it.

For me, the key idea is this: Our language—by its very structure, grammar, vocabulary—can direct (or motivate or dictate) our perceptions, thoughts, and behavior. There seems to be a link between language and action. The repercussions are important: it could mean that different languages embed different worldviews. In this way, language is not a medium to express universal ideas, but an active maker of ideas itself, an influencer on what kinds of ideas people make, what kinds of descriptions they create. Linguistic differences, then, become important in themselves. To put it crudely, if you use a language that has 1, 2, 3, and "many", you may well not remember the number of entities you observe beyond 3.

Now, to Pula's paper. He mentions that when Korzybski heard of Whorf's work, he was enthusiastic about it and recommended it to students and colleagues. Korzybski even invited Whorf to speak at the Second American Congress on General Semantics in 1941. Whorf agreed, but died in July of that year.

Pula also maintains that Korzybski came to the same idea as Whorf, independently in the 1920s, a decade before Whorf's published findings. He cites a passage in a 1924 paper where Korzybski writes about how human life is conditioned and limited by our use of symbols.

And Pula makes an interesting case that Nietzsche had the idea even earlier. He cites a passage where Nietzsche writes about the "the spell of certain grammatical functions" on our evaluations. Thus, Pula advocates, perhaps half-seriously, renaming the hypothesis the "Nietzsche-Korzybski-Sapir-Whorf Hypothesis" to get the priority right.

Neil Postman, another important GS teacher, noted how the hypothesis has gained traction in almost every field of learning—including physics, linguistics, philosophy, psychology and medicine. Postman also notes that it is still a "hypothesis" because no experiments have been devised to 'prove' it… which also makes the hypothesis controversial.

Anyway, Postman suggests—again, perhaps half-kidding—we refer to the hypothesis as the Sapir-Whorf-Korzybski-Ames-Einstein-Heisenberg-McLuhan-Et al. Hypothesis. He wrote this in his book *Teaching as a Subversive Activity*. And in the book he included an appendix, entirely of quotations from people who accept some version of Sapir-Whorf's hypothesis that language is not just a means of expression, but also the driver. And therefore, what we perceive and think about is a function of our language. It's an impressive compilation and shows why Postman wanted to add all those other names to the hypothesis.

To his end, Korzybski seemed to hold to the Sapir-Whorf hypothesis. He included a forceful statement of it in his last paper, "The Role of Language in the Perceptual Processes." He wrote: "We do not realize what tremendous power the structure of an habitual language has. *It is not an exaggeration to say that it enslaves us.* . . and that the structure which a language exhibits, and impresses upon us unconsciously, is automatically projected upon the world around us" [italics added].

Pula called it "one of his most brain-catching pithy expressions of this core notion of general semantics." I tend to agree. To me, Korzybski sums up why we should pay attention to the Sapir-Whorf Hypothesis. And it raises the stakes for GS generally. It gives us another reason to take special care in the words we use and how they "match up" with the territories they aim to describe and to be mindful of their influence on how we behave. And it's a fun idea to think about in any event.

Your Fellow Time-Binder,

Chris

Letter 26
The Observer and Observed

Dear Fellow Time-Binder,

We have to backtrack a bit to Heisenberg, uncertainty and an important point Korzybski made in *S&S*...

"Heisenberg's restricted principle of uncertainty is also the result of the application of non-elementalism," Korzybski wrote, "based on the observation that the 'observer' and the 'observed' cannot be sharply divided."

The basic idea here is that there is always an observer who makes an observation. Every description has a describer, every theory a theorist, every explanation an explainer. Consistent with GS principles of non-el, we should keep these pairs together. Just as there is no mind without a body, there is no observation without an observer.

The implications of this are numerous and profound. For our purposes, perhaps the most important is simply to note that the non-el character of observer/observed adds to, or in another way to think about, our general principle of uncertainty.

The observer-observed pairing also reminds me of Heinz von Foerster, who we met in an earlier letter. Foerster says: "Anything said is said by an observer." And, as a corollary: "Everything said is said *to* an observer."

Foerster is often affiliated with a loose affiliation of thinkers called "constructivists" and which includes, most notably, the psychologist Ernst von Glassersfeld, the biologists Humberto Maturanan and Francisco Verala, and the multi-disciplinary thinker Paul Watzlawick, among others. Foerster would chafe at being called a "constructivist" as most any creative thinker would chafe at any such label. Who wants to be pigeon-holed with a label?

In any event, while there are many differences between the thinkers so labeled, there are a few remarkable consistencies. If you've never read any of them, you are in for a treat. I would recommend Bernhard Poerksen's book *The Certainty of Uncertainty: Dialogues Introducing Constructivism*, as a good introduction. It is a collection of conversations, or interviews, with various "constructivists," including all the ones I named above.

Poerksen, in his introduction, writes that the common element for all of them is the idea that the observer plays a central role in any cognitive process. All descriptions are, in some sense, self-descriptions. They reveal the experiences, prejudices, preferences, etc., of whoever is making the observation. Any observation, description, etc., is filtered through a human nervous system. As photographer Dorothea Lange put it, "We see not only with our eyes but with all that we are and all that our culture is." As such, it cannot be 'objective' and "our craving for certainty and truth," as Poerksen writes, "is shattered."

Foerster, who has a way with aphorisms, captured the realization of this 'fact': "Objectivity is the subject's delusion that observing can be done without him."

Foerster has a wonderful puzzle that shows how the observer is intertwined with the observed. Consider the following:

"THIS SENTENCE HAS _____ LETTERS."

Foerster asks us to consider the missing word. There are two cool things about this puzzle. One is that there is more than one solution. And second, the solution itself is bound up in the puzzle itself—hence illustrating how an observer can be tangled up, inseparably, from the observed. Problems of this logical type are called "Eigenvalue problems," and the solutions are called "Eigenvalues." Our life, making observations and descriptions, is, in a sense, an Eigenvalue problem in action.

At one point in his conversation with Foerster, Poerksen asks if every observation is tied to an observer, then what do we do with such terms as 'fact,' 'reality,' and 'object.' Foerster's reply is that such terms "if used at all" would "only serve crutches, metaphors and shortcuts." They can help establish relations between different ideas, but any 'objectivity' is an illusion.

Foerster (and constructivists generally) pay a great deal of attention to language structure, as do those of us working with GS. For example, Forester points out how our language makes us passive agents of perception. In Lynn Segal's book *The Dream of Reality: Heinz von Foerster's Constructivism*, an excellent introduction to Foerster's thought, he uses the example of a lightbulb. We say the lightbulb emits light, thus implying it has an objective reality in the world. But light requires an observer—someone who can see and is in a position to see the light. Blind people cannot see light. This is just one example of several critiques on language, which I will not catalog here because they repeat much of what we've talked about already in these letters.

I mention the constructivists here because I find there is great affinity between constructivism and GS. The constructivists revel in their uncertainty and are fun to read. Another excellent book to introduce you to their way of thinking is *The Invented Reality: How Do We Know What We Believe We Know?*

edited by Paul Watzlawick, which contains a number of papers and essays on constructivist themes from a variety of disciplines. Constructivists, too, draw on a deep well of historical ideas and thinkers—including Vico, Berkeley, and Piaget.

And most of all, I am fascinated by the fact that Korzybski gave almost the exact formulation the constructivists often repeat: "All we know, and may know is a "joint phenomenon" of the observer and observed. Indeed there is no such thing as an "observer" without something to observe, nor such a thing as the "observed" without somebody making the observation" (*Collected Works*, p. 61).

Another really interesting thinker I would point you to is Adelbert Ames, Jr. (1835–1933). His work also shows how the individual is part of an environment; there is no truly isolated individual. And so our ideas and perceptions are likewise entwined with our environment.

Ames' particular interest was in physiological optics. He was one of the eighteen founding members of the Optical Society of America in 1916. And his life's work focuses on vision and researching different conditions, such as cyclophoria and aniseikonia. But he is most famous for constructing illusions.

Most people would trust what they see. Phrases such as "seeing is believing" and "I'll believe it when I see it" show how we place quite a bit of trust in what we see with our own eyes. Ames meant to cast some doubt about that.

Ames' experiments showed that people were active creators of what they "see." He wanted to show that our expectations have a great influence on what we see. As his biographer W.C. Bamberger put it: "Once the eye's supposed objectivity is disproved... knowledge and even reality begin to mean something more subjective and constructed."

For example, there is a famous chair demonstration. You look through a viewer with three peepholes. In each one, you see an assembly of wires that look like a chair. All three appear identical. Then you are instructed to look inside the box. And what you see is that two of the three "objects" you just viewed look like chairs, but the third is distorted beyond recognition. If you once again look in the peepholes, you will again see all three identical chairs.

Ames wrote that the experience shows "what you see does not correspond to what is 'out there,' does not exist out there and therefore cannot of itself be due to what is out there." The subject "fills in" the image of the chair, even one that doesn't exist, based on past experiences and expectations. It's really bizarre.

There were many more such illusions—rooms constructed in such a way that children looked bigger than their parents or where water seemed to run uphill or where playing cards seemed to change size right before your eye or where stationary balloons appear to be moving closer to you, etc.

The great takeaway from Ames is to debunk the idea that we "see" some kind of objective reality, that we're just passive receivers of images. Instead, we find—once again—the seer and the seen are bound together. We're fallible processors, or creators, and even something seemingly basic like what we "see" is highly subjective.

One last bit on this idea, from studies cited by Irving Lee:

- Subjects were asked to rank a series of colors from pleasant to unpleasant. Then they were given the same colors but with verbal descriptions attached such as "warm" "faded" "crude," etc. Twenty-five of the thirty-five subjects changed their ranking under the influence of the verbal tags.
- 1,484 people listened to two 'identical' pieces of classical music, but were not told they were identical. They were also given two sets of made-up quotes, from articles said to appear in music magazines, interpreting each piece. They were to match the music to the piece. Among the listeners, 67% of people preferred one piece over the other; 20% couldn't decide which they liked better but agreed they were different. Only 4% recognized the recording were the same.

We see here how we are greatly influenced by verbal labels. We let them do our thinking for us. They can alter what we see and hear and taste and feel. . . Beware of labels! And remember, every observation goes with an observer.

Your Fellow Time-Binder,

Chris

Letter 27

Causation

Dear Fellow Time-Binder,

The general principle of uncertainty covers a lot of ground, as you've noted. One thing you did not mention, but we should discuss, is the idea of causation.

People seem to love linking causes and effects. We link presidents with economic prosperity (or lack thereof), as if one caused the other. We say quarterbacks "won" Super Bowls. We believe Sally down the street is wealthy "because" she is a smart businessperson. We blame that guy who cut us off for getting us angry. And the faulty O-ring on the Space Shuttle caused it to blow up. And so on.

But can we say anything has a *single* cause? Korzybski taught we should at least think in terms of *a* cause, not *the* cause. Korzybski rejected two-valued causation in favor of ∞-valued causation; 'cause' and 'effect' do not correspond in a one-to-one relationship. Instead, there is a many-to-one relationship—many 'causes' bring about any single event.

Korzybski thought 'cause' and 'effect' were remnants of old two-valued logic and that careless use of these concepts leads to dogmatism and "other harmful semantic disturbances." The world we live in is constantly changing, as we have said. There are many things we don't know. And we can't grasp all the details. The number of potential influences, or causes, on any event is high.

So, in such a world, we would have to take into account everything, in all its details, to know that a certain 'cause' would lead to a certain 'effect.' This is something we cannot do. We can't really know if "cutting taxes will lead to x" because the number of variables is staggering and we can't repeat any experiment in exactly the same way.

As Korzybski says, this doesn't mean there are no regular patterns in life. What Korzybski is emphasizing is that 'same cause, same effect' is easily met with objections. To say that X leads to Y is an example of a two-valued orientation and one that is not similar in structure to the world in which we live. As Korzybski put it, "the term 'cause-effect'... is a primitive generalization never found in this world, as all events are *serially* related in a most complex way, independent of our way of speaking about them."

Instead, we must speak about probabilities, which are flexible. I think the greatest benefit of Korzybski's ∞-valued causation would be in the area of politics and religion. It always amazes me how sure people are that certain actions will lead to certain effects. Whether it is tax cuts, raising the minimum wage, or tariffs on Chinese goods—many people are far too sure of the effects of any policy.

I like to remind people of biological examples to show the consequences of simplistic cause-effect thinking. Stefano Mancuso writes about several of these in *The Nation of Plants*.

He takes an example from Darwin to highlight how relationships in nature can surprise us. Think of bumblebees and cats. You probably couldn't think of two animals more unrelated. And yet there is a clear relationship between the two. Mice are the enemies of bumblebees; they eat their larvae and destroy their nests. Cats kill mice. Thus, the enemy of my enemy is my friend. Darwin found that in villages where there are a lot of cats, there are also fewer mice. . . and more bumblebees.

"The ecological relationships that Darwin brings to our attention tell us of a world of bonds much more complex and ungraspable than had ever previously been supposed," Mancuso writes. "Relationships so complex as to connect everything to everything in a single network of the living."

In such a world, how can anyone be so sure of a simple cause-and-effect relationship. . . even between bumblebees and cats? It would be a mistake to assume that if you killed off the mice, you would have more bumblebees. The relationships of everything to everything else are enormously complex. Mancuso gives another example, where simple cause-effect thinking led to a disastrous policy.

In 1958, Mao and his government decided to target sparrows, which eat fruit and rice. Chinese scientists figured out that each sparrow ate ten pounds of grain per year. That meant for every million sparrows killed, China could save food for 60,000 people.

As part of a pest campaign, China marked sparrows as public enemy number one. The party campaigned to recruit citizens to combat these pests. Estimates vary, but the Chinese killed a huge number of sparrows.

Of course, the cause and effect relationships were more complex than "kill sparrows, equals more grain for people." Sparrows eat more than fruit and rice. Sparrows also eat bugs. The lack of sparrows meant the population of insects surged, including locusts. Immense swarms of locusts then destroyed much of China's crop. As Mancuso writes, from 1959 to 1961, "a series of ill-starred events partially related to natural disasters and partly caused by the mistaken reforms of the Great Leap Forward (the idea to exterminate the sparrows being one of the worst)[,] led to three years of famine so harsh that it caused the deaths of an estimated 20 to 40 million people."

It seems to me, a better appreciation for complexity (Korzybski's ∞-valued causation) would've nixed the idea of killing sparrows early.

Certainly, philosophers of all sorts, have doubted notions of cause and effect. I always think of a metaphor from Alan Watts. He says our view of cause and effect is as if we were peeking through a hole in a fence and we see a cat's head wander across our view followed by a tail. And then we see again the cat's head go back across the other way and the tail soon follows. Cause-and-effect reasoning would have us think the "head" caused the "tail." But they are just part of one process.

Nisargadatta Maharaj asks us to consider that there may be no causes—which is interesting, if only as a thought experiment. "Everything is uncaused," he says. "The world has no cause… Once you create for yourself a world in time and space, governed by causality, you are bound to search for and find causes for everything. You put the question and impose an answer."

And what to do with the idea that causes can *precede* effects?

In an article for *Quanta* magazine, Natalie Wolchover writes how physicists are observing indefinite causal order in numerous experiments. Robert Cottrell, editor of *The Browser*, comments that this is "a Wonderland-ish way of thinking about the world. Once we allow for the theoretical possibility of retroactive causality (we have no hard evidence that cause must precede effect, nor, indeed, any evidence that causality exists at all) we may come to see causality as a mutual relationship between events irrespective of time. 'A causes B' and 'B causes A' become 'simultaneously true.'"

The world of physics seems fairly far removed from our daily concerns, but it does show us that cause and effect are not a fact of nature. We may think, with David Hume, that causality is nothing but a "need of the human mind," a way for us to organize our experiences, but otherwise a flawed conception.

Flawed, but perhaps not irredeemable. Again, we can turn to our general principle of uncertainty and treat all such statements regarding cause and effect as fallible. We can use Korzybski's ∞-valued causation to talk about "causes." And we can rely on our other GS tools to keep us on the level here: For example, we can use English Minus the Absolutes and talk about how things *seem* to happen in a certain way… but always leave open the possibility that we have it wrong.

Your Fellow Time-Binder,

Chris

Letter 28

Fictions... or Abstractions

Dear Fellow Time-Binder,

Speaking of getting it 'wrong,' I should say that sometimes we get our descriptions 'wrong' on purpose. And it's fine.

Irving Lee devoted several pages in his book *Language Habits* to the idea that people often talk about events without caring how their description matches up with the 'facts' of experience. For one thing, this includes the area of fairy tales and fantasy. Think, too, of the great swath of art and literature based on intentionally fictionalized, or entirely made up, events. Movies, TV shows, etc. No sane person thinks Batman is 'real.'

So, there are times when we get our descriptions 'wrong,' and we know they are 'wrong,' but they are nonetheless useful for artistic, moral or other reasons. Vilhjalmur Stefansson (1879-1962), an explorer and ethnologist, wrote a light-hearted book about this called *Adventures in Error*.

Stefansson gives us many examples. One is the idea that the ostrich puts its head in the ground when it is scared. This ostrich exists as a fiction only. And yet it survives because it is useful. As Stefansson put it, "Our literature is richer, our vocabulary more picturesque through this beneficent bird of hypothesis."

He has many other examples, such as the stork that delivers babies, which "has ceased to be useful except in conversation with children, in the symbolism of the movie, and the picture postcard industry."

Or how we associate Siberia with cold. In the movies, Siberia is seemingly always cold. Yet, Siberia can also get very hot. Verkhoyansk, a Siberian town about 3,000 miles east of Moscow, holds the record for most widely varying temperature—from minus 90 Fahrenheit to 100.4 Fahrenheit. Siberia, generally, has warm but short summers.

Stefansson tells us an anecdote about how Tolstoy had the convicts in one of his novels die of sunstroke. The idea, though, was so out of whack with our idea of Siberia, that movie-makers changed the scene so the convicts froze to death instead.

As Stefansson writes, these few examples show the advantages of 'knowledge' easily grasped, picturesque and that has some moral value... even though they are, in a sense, 'faulty maps.'

Jeremy Bentham (1748-1832) pushed this idea further and said that language itself is impossible without fictions. C.K. Ogden (1889-1957) collected Bentham's writings on the theory of language in a book titled *Bentham's Theory of Fictions*. Ogden wrote, "Bentham believed that language must contain fictions in order to remain a language" because "a language which 'mirrored' reality would be impossible."

In this sense, I agree with Bentham—which is why I've emphasized in these letters that the answer to all of our maps is... another map, a 'better' map. The process has no end. There is no point we will ever reach and say, "Well, that's it. There is nothing more to be said." There is always more to say for the simple reasons we've banged on about in these letters—events are always changing, we can never know all there is to know, we always leave details out, etc.

There is another similar idea in *The Philosophy of 'As If'* by Hans Vaihinger (1852-1933), which we mentioned earlier. Vaihinger states the principle this way: "An idea whose theoretical untruth or incorrectness, and therewith its falsity, is admitted, is not for that reason practically valueless and useless; for such an idea, in spite of its theoretical nullity[,] may have great practical importance."

We know, for example, that Euclidean geometry uses idealized shapes that do not exist in the real world. Yet, we still use Euclidean geometry because it is useful enough for a variety of purposes. For example, if you want to carpet a room, Euclidean geometry gives you measurements sufficient for the task of figuring out how much carpet you'll need. Or Newtonian physics, which has been surpassed, but which we still use to send rockets to outer space.

Vaihinger goes through a bewildering array of examples in his book—systems of classification in the natural sciences, schematic drawings, legal fictions, countless philosophical concepts, etc.—and goes into far greater depth than we need to get into here. More important, I think, is to recognize the potential usefulness of fiction.

Korzybski knew about Vaihinger, and includes *The Philosophy of 'As If'* in the bibliography of *S&S* but he doesn't write anything about it in the book. I think there is a very good reason for this: Korzybski's GS already accounts for what we'd call "fictions," but Korzybski would call them "abstractions."

Raymond Rogers, in the summer 1950 edition of ETC, published "A Note on Vaihinger," which makes exactly this point. He writes, "it seems probable to me that, in Korzybski's terminology, most of Vaihinger's fictions would appear as 'Abstractions.'"

So, the knowing use of fictions, in Korzybski's GS, instead becomes "using a higher level abstraction." Suddenly, the whole thing doesn't seem so mysterious. We're just using the process of creating abstractions, and finding higher levels of abstractions useful.

I really like this re-casting of fiction, or error. Classification systems, then, are not "fictions" but abstractions. Likewise for Euclidean geometry.

Also, Korzybski's language adequately covers 'mistakes' such as saying the "grass is green," as Rogers points out. Instead, the grass seems green to me. But "as long as we have a keen awareness of the error we make in using the is'—as long as the error is deliberate, made only for practical reasons, as long as we are conscious of abstracting—we cannot, it seems to me, be greatly harmed in employing the 'is' of identity."

"Consciousness of abstracting" is one of the aims of Korzybski's GS. The idea that we know what we're doing protects us, in some measure, from assuming our abstractions are "truths"...

Your Fellow Time-Binder,

Chris

Letter 29
Media Ecology

Dear Fellow Time-Binder,

I have to tell you about another important figure in GS history—and someone who pointed a way forward for GS in an important talk, delivered in 1974, titled "Media Ecology: General Semantics in the Third Millennium." Three years later he became the editor of ETC, a post he held for ten years. He wrote many popular books, including a GS classic titled *Crazy Talk, Stupid Talk*. But he is probably best known for *Amusing Ourselves to Death*. He also contributed many articles and talks, which enrich our understanding of GS and related subjects.

I'm talking about Neil Postman (1931–2003). He started out as an English teacher. He never owned a computer and wrote all his books in longhand. Despite his Luddite tendencies, he frequently appeared on television, and you can watch several of these appearances on YouTube. Postman was a good writer with a sense of humor. His work has stood up well to the often unkind effects of time, and he has much to teach us today.

Let us start with his 1974 talk, which I like a lot.

Postman begins by recognizing Korzybski as a "brilliant and courageous explorer who charted some very mysterious and mystifying territory." Postman then summarizes in broad strokes what Korzybski's project was all about. He uses a quote from the physicist Arthur Eddington (also found in *S&S*), in which Eddington describes the theory of relativity in physics as reducing everything to relations—"that is to say, it is structure, not material, which counts."

In a similar way, Korzybski's GS is a relativity theory of language. It is the structure of language which Korzybski focused on, not the message itself. Postman calls this structure the "double helix of human communication," upon which we encode messages. Korzybski discovered the "genes"—such as multi-ordinality, self-reflexiveness and that problematic "is." For these discoveries, Postman thinks Korzybski should get a Nobel Prize.

But lest you think Postman is just shilling for Korzybski, he offers a pointed and highly interesting criticism on a blindspot in Korzybski's vision. In Postman's view, Korzybski neglected to consider the medium that carried our messages. He failed to see television, radio, film, etc., as languages of their own.

And so he did not see how these media impacted how people thought and what kinds of things they could say.

Postman says the best example of this oversight is found in one of Korzybski's own examples involving Roman numerals. You can't multiply 683 by 746 using Roman numerals. Korzybski says positional notation allows for this operation. And points out that positional notation has a definite structure.

What Postman alleges he misses is that positional notation presupposes the ability to write the problem down and see it. In this case, we have a writing system which makes it conceivable for us to multiply 683 by 746. But this is not the only example.

Postman points out that Korzybski makes almost no distinction between writing and speaking—yet both make definite demands on their users and keep them within certain boundaries. By not making distinctions between different media, Postman says that Korzybski treats these neuro-semantic environments as if they are all the same. He writes that Korzybski's lack of wonder about what effects TV or print or film or the telephone might have on the structure of communication "is almost incredible."

And this is where media ecology comes into play. "Media ecology is general semantics writ large," Postman says. And this phrase is oft-repeated by media ecologists and GS enthusiasts even today.

Media ecology begins with an appreciation that media itself is a language that has its own grammars and embed its own metaphysics. Media can dictate what we can say, and can't say, and thus how we relate to each other. One interesting example from Postman's talk: He says if you ask a stranger in an elevator "Are you visiting someone here and is it for business or pleasure?" You probably will have some trouble.

Why, Postman wonders, when strangers often ask this question on airplanes and get lengthy answers in response? If you say the difference has something to do with the fact that "an elevator ride takes no more than 60 seconds and an airplane ride takes no less than 60 minutes" then you are "giving the beginnings of a media ecological answer." Different environments make different interactions permissible. Media—the media ecologists insist—are environments.

On these ideas, Postman was much influenced by Marshall McLuhan (1911–1980). Though Postman is often credited with 'inventing' the term "media ecology," the work of media ecology has many predecessors. Perhaps the greatest of these is McLuhan, whose very name seems wrapped up with media ecology in the same way Korzybski's is with GS.

As Lance Strate wrote in his introduction to media ecology—fittingly titled *Media Ecology: An Approach to Understanding the Human Condition*—when he's asked what media ecology is, he usually responds with another question:

"Have you heard of Marshall McLuhan?"

McLuhan coined the famous aphorism "the medium is the message." His book *Understanding Media: The Extensions of Man* is a much-lauded classic, published in 1964. It is a hard book to describe. I can say it is dense in ideas, much like *S&S*. Reading it is like eating rich ice cream. You can only have so much of it in one sitting.

And it stays with you. I find myself thinking about what I read long after I've read it. McLuhan's ideas give you a new perceptual filter, a different way to consider the world around you. Ostensibly, the book is about media—though McLuhan's use of the term media is expansive. Media includes, of course, TV, radio, etc. But he also includes things like electric light.

In McLuhan's eyes, electric light is a medium. We can use electric light for night surgery or night baseball, it doesn't matter. These things are the "content" of electric light, but it is more important to recognize electric light as a medium, a medium without a message, but a medium nonetheless. And therefore it should be seen as part of our media landscape, just as TV, radio, etc., which shapes all of us in all kinds of ways.

In one of his more cryptic passages, McLuhan writes how GE thinks it's in the lightbulb business (remember this is c. 1964) but "it has not yet discovered that, quite as much as AT&T, it is in the business of moving information." Ponder that.

Anyway, the opening chapter covers his oft-quoted aphorism, "the medium is the message." I love this aphorism because, as with the best of aphorisms, it is open to a variety of interpretations and uses.

What does it mean?

Well, one thing it means is what I wrote earlier in this letter: the medium "shapes and controls the scale and form of human association and action." In other words, the medium itself has a great deal of influence on the kinds of messages we can create and on how we interact with each other.

Another Postman analogy: smoke signals. Such a medium limits what you can say. It's hard to talk about the nature of existence, for example. Smoke signals can communicate simple ideas, but it makes philosophy impossible.

Or consider Twitter. By its very structure, Twitter encourages certain kinds of messages and associations, and eliminates others. Similarly, users on YouTube, bound by a different set of constraints, create different messages and have different associations.

One of McLuhan's great insights is not to lose sight of the medium by simply looking at the content or message. He wants us to not just focus on what is being said (the message or content) but to think about how the message is encoded and carried (the medium).

Important in all this, is the idea that the medium forces changes regardless of the message. As McLuhan writes, automation altered our relations to one another—it changed work patterns, eliminated jobs, etc.—it didn't matter whether the factory "turned out cornflakes or Cadillacs." Our media work in the same way. It doesn't matter whether you approve of Twitter or not, you are bound by its constraints. The only way out is not to use it at all, but even then you will feel the effects as they ripple in the broader environment in which you live.

In another striking metaphor (he has gobs of them), McLuhan writes our media are like staples or natural resources (a metaphor pulled from the economist Harold Ennis, who had a large influence on McLuhan). We wouldn't question the idea that a country rich in oil or cotton would have some obvious social patterns of organization as a result. "Cotton and oil, like radio and TV, become 'fixed charges' on the entire psychic life of the community," he writes. "And this pervasive fact creates the unique cultural flavor of any society."

These changes or effects happen regardless of our intentions, or whether we approve of them or not. For McLuhan, media have a certain deterministic quality, they make certain things happen. He mocks the idea that media are somehow neutral. He would scoff at the statement that, say, "Facebook is neither good nor bad, it's what people do with it that counts." No.

Here's McLuhan:

> Suppose we were to say, "Apple pie is in itself neither good nor bad; it is the way it is used that determines its value." Or, "The smallpox virus is in itself neither good nor bad; it is the way it is used that determines its value."

These statements are obviously absurd. And McLuhan wants us to think of our media in a similar way; He doesn't want us to think the way media are used determines whether they are beneficial or not. He wants us to consider the nature of the medium itself... what does it dictate we do? Because the medium is the message.

To think otherwise is to fall into a Narcissistic trance. Narcissus, McLuhan reminds us, fell in love with an image that he failed to recognize as his own. (It is a common mistake to think Narcissus fell in love with himself.) The name "Narcissus" comes from the Greek for narcosis, meaning numbness. And for McLuhan, the story of Narcissus represented the typical numbness, or trance, that comes from using a technology/medium. We fall in love with the image (or extension) of ourselves, and thus we ignore how the medium alters our environment.

"Our conventional response to all media," McLuhan writes, "namely that it is how they are used that counts, is the numb stance of the technological idiot." For him, the content is like the meat a burglar uses to distract a dog and break into your house. The medium has the power to impose its own assumptions on you. "Docile acceptance of media" makes them "prisons without walls for their human users."

In summary: Media are environments. And new media create new environments. Environments are not "passive wrappings but active processes." Korzybski, it seems, missed this aspect of communication. But media ecology seems a sister discipline to GS—with many scholars conversant in one also conversant in the other—and well worth exploring. You can't go wrong with Postman and McLuhan to start.

Your Fellow Time-Binder,

Chris

Letter 30

Does GS Imply an Ethics

Dear Fellow Time-Binder,

You joke about achieving "GS enlightenment" but it does remind me of an idea I have thought about many times before. It's an answer to a question that runs something like this: "How does a person who has completely mastered all the principles of GS behave?" I mean, how does such a person—who is in command, at all times, of all these tools and ideas we've covered in these letters—think or act?

Other GS teachers have thought about this, too.

To start, as it seems we often do, let's see what Korzybski says in *S&S*:

> In general semantics we do not "preach" "morality" or "ethics" as such, but we train students in consciousness of abstracting, consciousness of the multiordinal of mechanisms of evaluation, relational orientations, etc., which bring about cortico-thalamic integration, and then as a result "morality," "ethics," awareness of social responsibilities, etc., follow automatically.

To Korzybski, passing off "noises" as legitimate symbols is "fraud." As he writes, "serious ethical and social results would follow from investigation of correct symbolism." So there seems no doubt where Korzysbki himself stands: GS does imply a certain kind of ethics, a certain sort of moral behavior.

Many GS teachers seem to agree.

Hayakawa, in his foreword to Rapoport's *Science and the Goals of Man*, points out that even science itself implies certain values—a preference for order over chaos, for 'truth' over 'lying,' for statements of verification versus authority. . . and even more basically, deciding what one should investigate over other possibilities involves a value choice, as does what evidence to admit, how to go about getting it, etc.

In a column in *ETC* ("The Non-Aristotelian Revision of Morality"), he goes through an excellent list of how someone who embraces GS would behave. Paraphrasing, such a person would:

- Never confuse a word with the thing.
- Always be aware of the ever-changing nature of everything.
- Constantly relate everything to everything else—i.e., everything "happens" in an environment.
- Always be aware of the similarity of dissimilar things, and the dissimilarity of similar things.
- Be aware of the pitfalls of either/or thinking.
- Know that we can never say all about anything, or know all about anything, which means such a person would not be dogmatic and capable of changing their minds in the fact of new evidence.
- Always be conscious of abstracting and aware of the levels of abstractions—remember the structural differential!

This is an ideal and requires quite a bit of self-discipline to achieve, if it is achievable at all. It may be that we can only hold to this as an ideal. As J. Samuel Bois put it, "General semantics is a long-range undertaking that will demand, first, a radical self-examination, and then, a painful self-administered change in the values and purposes each of us cherishes."

My favorite vision of what the ideal GS practitioner would be like is by Sanford Berman in a piece titled "Semantic Man." Berman's essay is an attempt to convey Irving Lee's own description of "what a 'semantic man' would look like if he were to apply the principles of general semantics to his own behavior." It is a profile of a GS Buddha.

Berman wrote it, too, as a tribute to his teacher Lee. The 'semantic man' is a fiction, "a mythical creation nowhere to be found in the world of reality. But if [Lee] had taken a closer look at himself he would have seen himself as others saw him—as the best example of the semantic man' we have had."

What would this 'semantic man' be like?

He would be a good listener and he would ask well-considered questions. He would not take words to mean what a dictionary says they mean; he knows meaning lies in people. He knows words can be used in "many different ways according to the experiences or even [the] whims of the user."

Berman says the ideal semantic man would be an eager collector of facts for evaluational use and would not dismiss new ideas. He is interested in learning and communicating, not in winning any "verbal fight."

Our ideal GS practitioner "will not confuse his inferences or assumptions with statements of fact." He will check his inferences against 'facts.' And here Berman makes a good point about how this does not mean "semantic man" is wishy-washy, as is often wrongly assumed:

"The 'semantic man' has deep convictions, assumptions, values, etc., but he understands that he must not hold these with a dogmatic 'know-it-all' attitude. He is always willing to listen with an open mind to the assumptions and beliefs of others, no matter how contrary they might be to his own. He respects, with dignity, the abstracting processes of others."

Our ideal person is one who is alive to all his senses, who is aware of his surroundings more than most. "I don't know, let's see" would be a personal motto.

Berman writes such a person is also aware of the misevaluations that come from anger, prejudice, fear, etc. He does not oversimplify. He does not think in terms of simple cause-and-effect. He uses the devices of GS to check his evaluations—the date, the index, the etc....

In my best moments, I like to think I get close to many of these ideals. I think it is worth the effort to try. To me, mastering the principles of GS expounded on in these letters leads to a calmer existence. I find I just don't get upset much over politics or sports or arguments with other people.

Think about national differences: What does it mean to be, say, a Mexican? Does it mean you were born in a certain geographical zone? What choice did anyone have in the matter? And think how abstract borders are. They are imagined. If you fly out in space and look at the Earth, you see a beautiful blue and green ball speckled with white clouds. There are no borders anywhere.

What does it mean to root for a certain sports team? As Jerry Seinfeld put it in one his bits, you're basically rooting for laundry. A player puts on a different shirt, you feel completely differently about that player. And I always chuckle at those sports fans who want to use "we" in talking about their teams. As in, "we won in Dallas last week." Not really, you didn't do a thing. You watched.

And what about politics? How does anybody know what the right policy is to pursue? Talk about abstractions—"economy" "taxes" "the middle class" "minorities" "business"—what does any of this mean, really?

This doesn't mean I don't have political opinions or can't enjoy sports or a good argument. It just means I recognize the abstractions involved. I appreciate the gulf that may exist between what I think and what other people think. And it's okay.

When I do get into arguments and discussions, my GS tools are invaluable. Words are just words, after all. They affect me only to the extent I allow them too. Otherwise, they are just noises. Messages don't even have to be in words—they include the nonverbal and messages we send by other means. How absurd is it to get upset because someone honks at me in their car? What is really happening there?

I love to read, and GS principles are analytical swords that cut through nonsense. I've become much better at taking apart texts and using GS to gain critical insights. Reading books or magazine articles, I can see weaknesses in the author's arguments as they may rely on fuzzy abstractions and generalizations. Using dates, indexing, etc.... Picking up on absolute terms, two-valued orientations, elemental language... all help me read with greater clarity.

GS principles have helped me appreciate the difficulty in knowing anything really. There is so much we can't know, and may never know. And we all have our own blind spots and biases and hopes and wishes and fears... We all have our own experiences and a set of inherited traits, etc. All these things filter what we perceive.

As a result, GS principles have made me much more sympathetic to other people generally. Being mindful of abstractions is hard, especially hard in a culture that seems to value them so highly—think of the emotional charge that surrounds political debates, sporting events and religious differences. But all of these things involve high-level abstractions far removed from the world of experience, as we've noted.

GS helps me resist certain traps that society sets for the unwary. The most insidious of these is advertising. We are bombarded with advertising. I try to look away, but it's impossible in our society to not be exposed to heavy amounts of ads. And it may be that we can't immunize ourselves totally against their hypnotic effects. GS principles, though, can help—I see ads nowadays and when I can't look away, I always ask myself questions about what the ad is trying to say... that if I drink a certain kind of vodka... or drive a certain kind of car... all these wonderful experiences await? This self-questioning is best done in a somewhat mocking tone.

Political slogans are another area where GS principles make it easier to resist. "Make America Great Again" and "Build Back Better" become meaningless nonsense. What do each of these refer to? They refer to super high-level abstractions, only marginally tethered to anything 'real.' You'll marvel that anyone took them seriously, much less why people put such things on hats and bumper stickers. The absurdity of it all will make you laugh.

GS will help you see life, the universe and everything (as Douglas Adams would have it) as an experiential whole. People love to chop up the world of experience into disciplines and subjects. This is "physics," that is "psychology," etc. This is "work," that is "play." This is "American" and that is "Chinese." But GS will give you an X-ray-like vision to see past these distinctions, ask good questions, and see the connectedness of all events.

Finally, I will say that GS can help you appreciate common things and ordinary experiences more than you did before. Even a simple walk through the woods will have me reflecting on how the world is always changing, how you yourself are changing, how you (as an observer) are an active 'creator' of what you observe, how you can never perceive it all, etc.

In summary, I think being a practitioner of GS brings many, many rewards.

Your Fellow Time-Binder,

Chris

Letter 31

Final Letter and Summing Up

Dear Fellow Time-Binder,

It is time to sum up the Korzybskian system of general semantics, as we've covered it in these letters. In this effort, we will turn to Marjorie Kendig (1892–1981), or simply "M. Kendig," as she called herself. She was an important figure in GS history, who I mentioned earlier and who had a great grasp of what Korzybski aimed to achieve. She was master of his system and she kept the Institute afloat after his death by assuming the leadership role.

An entire issue of the *General Semantics Bulletin*, 84 pages, was given over to remembering her upon her death. It's filled with warm memories and appreciation. She lived general semantics and really dedicated most of her life to it.

As Charlotte Read wrote in a biographical sketch of Kendig: "[She was born in] 1892. She lived for 89 years, 5 months and 39 days. She wanted to live her life to the brim, and this she did in overflowing measure. For her, 'life'—the last forty-seven years of it—was at the center of the general semantics world. She was largely instrumental in creating that world."

After graduating from Vassar College in 1915, she started her career in publishing at Charles Scibners' Sons in New York. In 1918, she joined the Vassar Nurse Training Camp to help in the war effort. After the war, she returned to publishing.

In 1931, she left publishing to work at the American College for Women in Geneva, Switzerland, as Assistant to the Director. She also did graduate work in 1932 at the University of Geneva, where she took courses with the famed Swiss psychologist Jean Piaget.

Back in the US in 1933, she married, divorced and completed a master's degree in education at the Teachers College of Columbia University. In 1934, she accepted a position at the head of the Barstow School for Girls in Kansas City. While there, she heard of Korzybski's *Science & Sanity*. The reading made a deep impression, and she wrote to Korzybski, then living in Brooklyn. They arranged to meet in August, and meet they did.

Kendig tried to bring GS insights to the curriculum at Barstow. She wanted her teachers trained in its use. And she invited Korzybski to give lectures.

Kendig had great respect and deep admiration for Korzybski.

When Korzybski founded the new Institute of General Semantics in 1938, Kendig left Barstow to become its Educational Director. She was also a Founding Trustee and Secretary of the Board. The small institute, initially financed by Corenelisu Crane, began with Korzybski, Kendig, and Pearl Johnecheck (Korzybski's assistant). Kendig's knowledge of publishing, marketing, and education were critical to the fledgling institute.

As one teacher of GS remembered, "the Institute of General Semantics, its members, students, friends, trustees, etc., were her family and 'tribe.' It was what made her as 'happy' as she could ever be."

Upon Korzybski's death in 1950, she became director. The Institute, at that time, operated out of a large house in Lime Rock, Connecticut. Reading over the history of the Institute, I get the feeling she was the glue that held the thing together. Kendig's personality also pops from the page.

She loved cats. At Lime Rock, the Institute's cat population ran from ten to twenty, and, with the exception of one or two housecats, the rest lived outside the walls of the house. She knew all their names.

One of her favorite expressions, which she used when people came to her with problems was "Do you want me to hold your hot little hand, darling?" As one writer remembered, the expression was part of her way of teaching GS. "There is no 'reality' 'out there,' it's your doing, and you will have to face it yourself, for there is no 'authority' no 'truth' and no certainties in this ever-changing world. And you can do it yourself; you're doing it that way anyway, now all you have to do is accept the fact."

Kendig was a good writer herself, and I would've loved for her to write the book she long wanted to write, but for which her many other responsibilities seemed to preclude. What we have from her—memos, prefaces, etc.—is quite good.

In an introduction to a Korzybski paper, she used a memorable metaphor to explain an "inadequate evaluation." Kendig wrote about how a frightened rabbit will freeze in the middle of a field and thus escape detection from predators. But the 'same' rabbit in the middle of a road frightened by oncoming headlights will make the same evaluation. "The 'meaning' to the rabbit may be said to be the 'same' in both 'contexts'" Kendig wrote, ``but his survival evaluation is inadequate to the second empirical situation." Part of what GS helped people to do was think more clearly about their evaluations and to appreciate no two events are ever exactly alike.

Another remembrance recalled something Kendig said—which she may or may not have said exactly this way, but I like to think she did, it fits:

> Too many people get trapped into the picture they think they are presenting to others. Why I, I have absolutely no self-image of myself. I am what I am. I believe what I believe. I have no idea what Image I project to other people. But since I approve of myself and what I'm doing, why should I care? I assume that others will see me as I am, and since I don't wish to be otherwise, that's the way it has to be. Do what you think should be done, and don't worry about whatever abstraction you create in other people's minds.

In my readings, I have come to think of Kendig as someone with high standards for GS scholarship and thinking and greatly adept at using the system herself. Be that as it may, she was also quite aware that you couldn't be a puritan about it. She recognized, and wrote about, how you want to be able to express yourself intensionally *and* extensionally.

We must use words to talk and we can't point at everything. Intensional, remember, means to rely on 'dictionary definitions.' It also means to talk about, say, 'people.' Extensional would be to talk about person$_1$, person$_2$, person$_3$, etc. You cannot be extensional all the time. "NEVER PURE," Kendig wrote in all caps. "But when we speak of our attitudes, then we should have the extensional attitude, which means use extension predominantly. Extension itself is defined by intension [that is, verbally]. This circularity is everywhere present and unavoidable, and all 'Puritanism' is a delusion."

Kendig, despite her own high level of attainment with GS, remained remarkably humble. Her words on this point are striking and worth quoting in full. From a note in 1968:

> The last thing I would call myself is a 'general semanticist.' I haven't the vaguest notion what the term represents to a person who uses it. I would have to question him/her in a rather thoroughgoing way. After 34 years of study, training and self-training, editing, and teaching, I feel only mildly secure or justified in labeling myself a 'non-Aristotelian' or, to make it more limited, a 'Korzybskian.' So far as my experience goes, I would guess that I have known about 30 individuals who have in some degree adequately, by my standards, mastered this highly general, very simple, very difficult system of orientation and method of evaluating— reversing as it must all our 'cultural conditioning'. . ."

Her sharp words leave a sting—ever since reading them, I am reluctant to call myself a 'general semanticist,' or to feign mastery of GS. I would be slightly embarrassed to do so.

This is just a sampling of Kendig's writing, who used words like scissors, cutting away at pretension, misevaluation, and ambiguity. I could quote her all day. But we must move along.

Kendig is good to mention at this point in our correspondence, because she had a way of summing up what GS is all about and describing the system. She had a deep understanding of GS and how it fit.

What are we talking about when we talk about "Korzybski's non-Aristotelian system and general semantics"? She hit those points as if she had repeated them a thousand times; we're talking chiefly about being conscious of our abstractions, the various levels of abstractions and the use of extensional devices (dating, indexing, etc.).

We're talking about an open-ended system, a fact that Kendig thought was much unappreciated. We'll continue to make new 'maps'—ideas, theories, formulations, etc.—but the principles of GS still apply to these new word pictures.

Wendell Johnson called GS a new "perceptual filter." He thought it was a good way to help us cope with the world we live in, characterized by change.

I think of GS as a practical philosophy. Korzybski himself could be rough on philosophers, who he seemed to regard as mostly unscientific and playing word games. But he still included a bunch of philosophers in his dedication to *S&S*. And he read Wittgenstein, loved the aphoristic style of the *Tractatus* and enjoyed quoting it to others. He and his wife Mira would read passages of the *Tractatus* to each other in bed.

Certainly, many if not all of Korzybski's main concerns have found expression in the works of great philosophers. In particular, in the 20th century, one may find common threads with Korzybski's GS in the likes of Bertrand Russell, Ludwig Wittgenstein, J.L. Austin, W.O. Quine, and others. (Quine actually attended Korzybski's seminars.) But while they shared many of the same concerns as Korzybski they did not teach GS. As I said at the start of these letters, GS has a set of tools and a way of cohering together into a system that make it unique and worth preserving in its own right, as a kind of applied epistemology.

So, to sum up: We've covered a lot of ground and you've added many tools to your evaluation toolkit. I hope you've enjoyed our correspondence as much as I have. And I hope you will apply general semantics and find it a life-enriching pursuit.

Your Fellow Time-Binder,

Chris

Author Biography

Christopher W. Mayer is an independent scholar and the Co-founder and Portfolio Manager of Woodlock House Family Capital, an investment firm based in Mount Airy, Maryland. He is the author of several popular books on investing, including *100 Baggers: Stocks That Return 100 to 1 and How to Find Them*. As an enthusiast of Korzybski and general semantics he also wrote *How Do You Know? A Guide to Clear Thinking About Wall Street, Investing and Life*, which received the S.I. Hayakawa Book Award from the Institute of General Semantics in 2019.

Acknowledgements

I would like to thank Lance Strate, President of the Institute of General Semantics for giving me access to the archives of ETC and the General Semantics Bulletin. These were especially invaluable resources in helping to flesh out some of the personalities in the General Semantics universe.

I would like to thank the Institute of General Semantics for all its efforts to keep Korzybki's ideas alive and for giving me the opportunity to contribute. I would especially like to thank Lance, Corey Anton, Thom Gencarelli and Marty Levinson for their encouragement and support of my work.

Index

Note: Page numbers in italics indicate figures or tables.

absolutes, elimination of, 74–78
absolutist thinking, helpful phrases to avoid, 75–76
abstracting/abstractions, 35–36, 38, 40–43, 47, 53, 89, 111, 113, 115, 141–142, *142*, 150, *151*
abstractions, vs. fictions, 140–142
Adams, Douglas, 7, 151
Advaita Vedanta, 111
Allen, Steve, 63
Ames, Adelbert, Jr., 135–136
anti-Semitism, 22
Anton, Corey, 108–109
Aquinas, Thomas, 55
Aristotelian categories, 87, 118
Aristotelian logic, 55–58, *56*, 86, 90, 102, 118
Aristotle, 55, 59, 61
assumptions, 15, 26, 55, 65, 81, 87–88, 113, 114, 115, 116–117, 124
ataraxia, 78
Aua, 121
Austin, J.L., 156
author biography, 157
Axelrod, Robert, 93–94

Bacon, Francis, 59–61, *61*, 87
Bakewell, Sarah, 78
Bamberger, W.C., 135
Baron, Rebekah, 123
Bateson, Gregory, 59
Beer, Stafford, 59
Bentham, Jeremy, 117, 141
Berkeley, George, 135
Berman, Sanford I., 51–52, *53*, 149, 150
Bhava, 111

'biology,' 68
Bois, J. Samuel, 65, 89–91, 149
Bourland, D. David, Jr., 79
Bronowski, Jacob, 128
Buffett, Warren, 107, 122
Burroughs, William S., 63

Carpenter, Edmund, 46, 80, 121
causation, 137–139, *139*
cause-effect thinking, 137–139
chain index, 26–29
Chase, Stuart, 16, 64
China, 138–139
Chisholm, Francis, 27, 63
classification systems, 142
conclusions, 118
constructivists, 69, 133–134, *134–135*
context, 26–28
Cottrell, Robert, 139
Crane, Cornelius, 63
cross-binding, 84
crossbinds, 53–54, 72
Cybernetics, 59

Darwin, Charles, 115, 138
dates, 18–21, 33, 72, 127, 128
delayed reactions, 112–113
demoralization, 104–109
Descartes, René, 59, 61, 67, 115
description level, 41
descriptions, 71–72, 97–98, *98*, 133, *134*, 140
Dewey, John, 12, 59, 117
dogmatism, 137, 150
"double helix of human communication," 143
dualism, 67–69

Ecology of Mind, 59
Eddington, Arthur, 143
Edgerly, Mira, 10, 14
Ehrenberg, Rachel, 25
"Eigenvalue problems, 134
"Eigenvalues," 134
Einstein, Albert, 26–27, 58, 97
either/or thinking, 83–86, 99
elementalistic (el) thinking, 67–69
Eliot, Thomas, 55
Ellis, Albert, 81
empathy (EM), 72–73
"English Minus Absolutes" (EMA), 74–78, 79, 82, 83, 118, 128
Ennis, Harold, 145
'environment,' 68
epoché, 78, 113
E-Prime, 79–82
erligion, 98
error, 141–142
etc., 30–32, 127
ETC., 30, 55, 64, 68, 83, 95, 108, 123, 141, 143, 148
ethics, general semantics and, 148–152
Euclid, 55, 58
Euclidean geometry, 58, 99–100, 141, 142
evaluation(s), 15–16, 35, 54, 69, 112–113, 150, 154
event level, 34–35, 41
events, 35, 37, 140
evidence, 103
"experiential level," 110
extension, 155
extensional definitions, 88, 91–92, 95
extensional devices, 70, 72–73
extensional questions, 120

facts, 87, 134
    fact-finder, 47–54
    vs. inferences, 49–53, *49*
"false to facts," 46
falsity, 99–103

fascism, 84
fate, logical, 114–119
fiction, language and, 140–142, *see also* abstractions
fictionalism, theory of, 116–117
fictions, vs. abstractions, 140–142
Foerster, Heinz von, 69–70, 133, 134
French, James, 53–54, 82, 91–92
frustration, 104–109
Frydman, Maurice, 26
Fuller, Buckminster, 18–19, 25, 29, 31, 52, 63, 68, 99
fun questions, 120, 121

game theory, 93–94
Gautama the Buddha, 111
generalizations, 34–35, 37, 103, 115
general principle of uncertainty, 124–128, *see also* uncertainty
general semantics (GS), 7, 14–19, 21, 47–48, 156
    after Korzybski's death, 65–66
    as "another kind of algebra," 70–71
    Aristotelian logic and, 55–56
    dualism and, 67–69
    either/or thinking and, 56
    etc. and, 30–32
    ethics and, 148–152
    evaluation and, 15–16
    evolution of, 17
    facts vs. inferences and, 49–51
    "false to facts" and, 46
    heyday of, 63–64
    history of ideas and, 87
    introducing, 13–17
    maps and, 44–45, 107
    media ecology and, 144
    multi-valued thinking and, 85–86
    as non-Aristotelian system, 58–59
    as non-verbal discipline, 112
    as "perceptual filter," 156
    popularizations of, 64
    as practical philosophy, 156
    as relativity theory of language, 143

rewards of, 150–152
roots of, 78
self-discipline and, 149
sense of humor and, 52
silence and, 110–113
therapeutic value of, 106, 110–113
tools of, 18–21, 22–24, 27, 30–32, 33, 150–151
uncertainty and, 71, 124–128
Zen Buddhism and, 108–110
General Semantics Bulletin, 48, 68, 74, 79, 91–92, 125, 153
Glassersfeld, Ernst von, 69, 133
Gödel, Kurt, 58
Great Depression, 62
Grimes, John Allen, 111
"GS enlightenment," 148

Hallie, Phillip, 78
Harrison, W. Benton, 62, 64–65
Haslam, Gerald W., 84
Haslam, Janice E., 84
Hayakawa, S.I., 63, 64, 83–86, 88, 95, 105, 112, 113, 148
Heinlein, Robert, 63
Heisenberg, Werner, 58, 126, 128, 133
Hicks, Bill, 36
higher-level abstractions, 35–36
Hitler, Adolf, 48, 84, 85, 128
Hobbes, Thomas, 45, 59, 79, 87, 93, 115
Horowitz, Gad, 28, 40–41, 72–73
Hume, David, 139
humility, 38
humor, 42–43
hyphens, 72, 127

idealism, 10, 104–109
idols of the cave, 60
idols of the marketplace, 60
idols of the theater, 60
idols of the tribe, 60
IFD disease, 104–109
imagination, 98
Incompleteness Theorem, 58

indeterminateness, 99–103, 101
indexing, 22–25, 33, 72, 127, 128
inference level, 34–35, 41
inferences, 34–35, 37, 38, 71, 98
  vs. facts, 49–53, *49*
infinite-valued orientation, 85–86
Institute of General Semantics (IGS), 30, 79, 89
  ambitions of, 64
  establishment of, 63, 154
intension, 155
intensional definitions, 88, 91–92
intensional devices, 70
intensional questions, 120
International Society for General Semantics (ISGS), 64
"invariance," 96
invariants, 96–97, 101

James, William, 117
Jaroszewski, Irene, 124
Jesus, 111, 115
Johnson, Mark, 59
Johnson, Wendell, 14–15, 38, 56, 58, 63, 64, 87, 102–103, 104–107, 110–112, 119–120, 121–123, 156
judgment, suspension of, 78, 112–113

Kant, Immanuel, 117
Kauffman, Draper, 69
Kendig, Marjorie, 14, 61, 64, 65, 153–156
Keyes, Kenneth, Jr., 75–76
Keyser, Cassius J., 22, 114–115, 118, 119
Kierkegaard, Søren, 111
Kiki, 14
Kodish, Bruce, 9, 22, 27, 28, 33, 65–66, 81–82, 84, 125
Kodish, Susan Presby, 74, 81–82, 125
Korzybski, Alfred, *13*, 15–16, 46, 53, 63, 156
  abstracting and, 142
  after *Science & Sanity*, 62–66
  anti-Semitism and, 22

Aristotelian logic and, 55–56, 58
Bacon and, 59–61, 61
biography of, 9–10, 84
Bourland and, 79, 80
on causation, 137–138
causation and, 139
constructivists and, 135
death of, 65, 89, 154
Descartes and, 61
diagrams of, 116
documentary films on, 75
either/or thinking and, 86
error and, 142
extensional definitions and, 95
extensional orientation and, 70, 74
"Fate and Freedom," 115–116
formulates GS as non-Aristotelian, 86
general semantics (GS) and, 47–48
Harrison's description of, 64–65
Hayakawa and, 83–84, 95
Heisenberg and, 126
on imperfection, 113
Johnson and, 104–105
Kendig and, 153–154
Keyser and, 114–115, 118
"Korzybski's Happiness Formula," 108
Lee and, 47–48, 88–89
on logical fate, 115–116, *116*
Manhood of Humanity, 10–11, 12, 17, 37, 60, 61, 65, 84, 114
on maps, 44–45
May and, 67
natural order of evaluation and, 35–36
Nietzsche and, 129, 131
non-Aristotelian systems and, 55–56
on objective level, 110
Olivet College lectures, 16, 63
over/under defined terms and, 88
philosophy and, 156
Postman and, 143–144
Pula and, 125–126
Rapoport and, 94–95, 99
"Release of Atomic Energy," 84–85
"The Role of Language in the Perceptual Processes," 132
roots of GS and, 78
safety devices and, 70
Sapir-Whorf hypothesis and, 129–132
Science & Sanity, 17, 18, 30, 33, 38, 41–42, 55, 58, 61, 62–66, 79, 94, 100, 104–107, 116, 124–126, 141, 143, 148, 153
self-evaluation and, 22
sense of humor, 42–43
structural differential and, 38, 40, *40*
supporters and followers of, 47
time-binding and, 9–12, 25, 36–37, 38
"Time-Binding": The General Theory," 38
uncertainty and, 124, 128
Vaihinger and, 141
Whorf and, 131
work ethic of, 64–65
"working devices" and, 17, 21, 30, 33
Yale seminar, 65
"Korzybski's Happiness Formula," 108

labels, 24–25, 136
Lakoff, George, 59
Lange, Dorothea, 134
language, 111, 114
    action and, 131
    fiction and, 140–141
    Hitler's use of, 48
    influence on perceptions, thoughts and behavior, 131, 132
    as map, 44–45
    relativity theory of, 143
    spelling, 76–77
    structure of, 134

vocabulary choices, 74–76, 79
Wittgenstein's philosophy of, 58
words we should do without, 77, 79
Lapidus Principle, 119
Law of Identity, 56
Law of Noncontradiction, 57–58
Law of the Excluded Middle, 56–57, 102
Lee, Irving, 15, 46, 47–53, 63, 64, 87, 88–89, 136, 140, 149
Levinson, Martin, 63
Linguistic Relativism, 58
Locke, John, 87
Logical Fate, 114–119, *117*, 119
Longstreet, Ethel, 90–91
lower-level abstractions, 35–36

MacNeal, Edward, 68–69
Maharaj, Nisargadatta, 26, 28, 139
Maharshi, Bhagavan Sri Ramana, 110–111
Maloney, Martin, 49
Mancuso, Stefano, 138
Mao Zedong, 138
map(s), 81, 141
general semantics (GS) and, 44–45
vs. territory, 43, 44–46, 98, 107
Martinich, A.P., 59
Maslow, Abraham, 63, 74
'mathematics,' 68
Maturanan, Humberto, 133
maximum motivation (MM), 108
May, Rollo, 67, 69, 80
Mayper, Stuart, 81, 119
McLuhan, Marshall, 59, 144–147
meaning, quest for, 96–97
meaninglessness, 99–103, 101–102
Media Ecology, 59, 143–147
Metaphor Theory, 59
mind/body dualism, 67
minimum expectations (ME), 108
Modupe, Prince, 46
Montaigne, Michel de, 78
Morgan, Augustus de, 79
Morris, Charles, 108

multi-ordinality, 89–90
multi-valued thinking, 85–86
Munger, Charlie, 107, 122

Narcissus, 145
natural order of evaluation, 35
Nazism, 22, 84, 128
Neal, David, 25
neuro-linguistic inevitability, 114
Newton, Isaac, 55, 58, 61, 97
Newtonian physics, 58, 141
Nietzsche, Friedrich, 129, 131
non-additivity, 100, 102
non-allness, principle of, 30–32, 56
non-Aristotelian systems, 42, 55–61, *56*, 69, 86, 99, 156
non-elementalistic (non-el) thinking, 67–69, 133
non-Euclidean geometries, 100
non-GS, 55
non-Newtonian physics, 58
nonverbal world, 103

objective level, 110
objectivity, 135, 136
object level, 34–35, 41
observations, 133–136, 134
observed, observer and, 133–136
observer, observed and, 133–136
Ogden, C.K., 117, 141
open-ended systems, 156
operational philosophy (OP), 93–98, 101–102
operational questions, 120
'organism,' 68
Osborne, Arthur, 51–52

parabola, 34–35, 40–42, *42*, 47
pathology-inducing questions, 120, 121–122
'philosophy,' 68
physics, 97, 139
Piaget, Jean, 135, 153
Pilate, 111

Plato, 67, 115
Poerksen, Bernhard, 133–134
politics, 98, 150, 151
Postman, Neil, 59, 131, 143–145
prejudice, 22–23, 113, 134
premises, 118
Principle of Tolerance, 128
prisoner's dilemma, 93–94
probabilities, 138
probability, 128
process, 18–21, 33
Pseudo-Dionysius the Areopagite, 111
Pula, Robert, 14–15, 41–42, 49–50, 53, 63, 65, 108, 114, 118, 120–122, 124–128, 129, 131, 132
Pyrrho, 78
Pythagorean Theorem, 99

quantum mechanics, 97
quantum physics, 58
questions
how to ask, 119–123
recasting, 122–123
Quine, W.O., 156
quotation marks, single, 68, 71, 72, 127

Rapoport, Anatol, 88, 93–98, 99, 100–102, 148
Rasmussen, Knud, 121
Read, Allen Walker, 74–77, 79
Read, Charlotte Schuchardt, 62, 64, 74, 153
Relational Communication, 59
"relativity of meaning," 96
Rogers, Raymond, 141–142
Rorty, Richard, 97, 98, 117
Russell, Bertrand, 80, 156

safety devices, 67–73
Santayana, George, 80
Sapir, Edward, 58, 129–132
Sapir-Whorf hypothesis, 129–132
Schopenhauer, Arthur, 106
Segal, Lynn, 134

Seib, Gerald, 20
Seinfeld, Jerry, 150
self-deception, benefits of, 117
self-descriptions, 134
self-discipline, 149
"semantic man," 149–150
"semantic reaction," 16
Seneca, letters of, 7
Sextus Empiricus, 78
Sies, Luther, 105
silence, 110–113
"similar in structure" (SiS), 44–46, 70
Skepticism, 78
Snyder, Robert, 31
Society for General Semantics, 64
Socrates, 106
space-time, 67–68
speculative questions, 120–121
spelling, 76–77
Spinoza, Baruch, 115
State, Lance, 55
Stefansson, Vilhjalmur, 140
Stevenson, Helen, 48–49
Stewart, Joseph, 105
Stockdale, Steve, 74
Strate, Lance, 144–145
structural differential (SD), 34, *34*, 98, 111
    as "anthropometer," 38
    general semantics (GS) and, 41–42
    introducing, 33–39
    models of, *34*, 38–39, 40–42, *40*, *42*
    variations on, 40–43
Suzuki, D.T., 108
syllogisms, 57, 69
system(s), 69–70, 86
    definition of, 69
    nested, 70
    open-ended, 156
    "symbol systems," 14–15
    systems within, 70
systems thinking, 69–70

territory, vs. map, 43, 44–46, 98, 107

Theory of Relativity, 58
things, vs. words, 42, 44, 87
thinking-feeling, 68
time, 95–96
time-binding, 25, 36–37, 38
　errant, 103
　essence of, 33–34
　extensional definition of, 91–92
　"good" vs. "bad," 53–54
　intensional definition of, 92
"tit-for-tat" strategy, 93–94
tolerance, 128
Tolstoy, Leo, 140
'truth,' 72, 99–103, 117–118
two-valued orientations, 85–86

uncertainty, 133–134
　embracing, 71
　general principle of, 124–128, 137, 139, see also Uncertainty Principle (Heisenberg)
Uncertainty Principle (Heisenberg), 58, 126, 133
Uncertainty Umbrella, 124, 127–128, *127*, 128
unhappiness, 107
"unsayable" level, 110
the unspeakable, 35
usefulness, 117–118

Vaihinger, Hans, 116–117, 141
validity, vs. truth, 101
Vaskalin, 111
Verala, Francisco, 133
verbalisms, 103
Vico, Giambattista, 135

Wanderer, Robert, 14–15
Watson, Richard, 61
Watts, Alan, 19–20, 28, 71, 139
Watzlawick, Paul, 59, 107, 133, 135
Weinberg, Harry, 112
Weinberg, harry, 21, 51, 100
"what is going on" (WIGO), 34, 37

Whitehead, Alfred North, 77–78, 80
Whorf, Benjamin, 58, 129–132
Wiener, Norbert, 59
Wilson, Robert Anton (RAW), 63, 80, 81, 111
Wittgenstein, Ludwig, 58, 156
Wolchover, Natalie, 139
words, 115
　ambiguous, 88–90
　assumptions underlying, 87–88
　effects of using, 87
　meaning of, 87–92, 93, 114
　multi-ordinal character of, 89–90
　over/under defined, 88, 90
　vs. things, 42, 44, 87
"working devices," 17, 18–20, 22–24, 27, 30–32, 33, 70, 127
World War I, 84
World War II, 47–48, 53, 84, 85, 128

X-Files, 97

Zagorin, Perez, 59
Zen Buddhism, 108–110

www.ingramcontent.com/pod-product-compliance
Lightning Source LLC
Chambersburg PA
CBHW060156050426
42446CB00013B/2850